what neXt?

Connecting your ministry with the generation formerly known as X*

Augsburg Fortress
Minneapolis

What NeXt?

Connecting Your Ministry
with the Generation Formerly Known as X*

Scripture quotations, unless otherwise noted, are from New Revised Standard Version Bible, copyright © 1989, Division of Christian Education of the National Council of the Churches of Christ in the United States of America.

The opening story in chapter 1, "A New Generation," was provided by Carl Sharon, campus pastor, New Haven, Conn.

Editors: Andrea Lee Schieber, Ann Terman Olson
Cover design: Barb Roth
Cover photograph: Tony Stone Images, Inc.
Project team: Bill Huff, Andrea Lee Schieber, Richard Webb
Developed in cooperation with the Division for Congregational Ministries of the Evangelical Lutheran Church in America, Richard Webb, project manager.

This book has a companion videocassette resource, What NeXt? Video 0-8066-3969-5. Order copies from Augsburg Fortress, 800-328-4648.

Manufactured in the U.S.A.   AF -9-3968

99   00   01   02   03   04   1   2   3   4   5   6   7   8   9   10

contents

foreword

*I*n the course of developing this book and deciding upon its title, one thing became clear: This generation does not favor the moniker "Generation X." Yet that's the name most of us know for this age-group. What to do? Our solution was to try to please everyone—to respect the concerns of the generation and to choose a familiar descriptor for our readers—and not to take it all too seriously. Hence, the subtitle, lengthy as it is: Connecting Your Ministry with the Generation Formerly Known as X.

Throughout this book you will find that the writers of *What NeXt?* accommodated the editorial desire for clarity and brevity. For the most part, they use the term "Generation X" when referring to this age cohort. Increasingly the term "postmodern" is also being used; many prefer the term because it includes people of any age who share characteristics shaped by postmodern thinking and culture. Certainly, the practitioner-writers of this book have found that in designing ministry to connect with Generation X, they are in fact connecting with a whole host of people for whom the church has been unfamiliar or even unwelcoming.

So, what next? What shape will the church's connection with Generation X take? Our objective in publishing this book is to help you, a motivated congregation leader, to learn a few things from the experience of others in ministry with the generation. Janet M. Corpus sets the stage with God's call to us. In "A New Generation" Christine L. Reifschneider addresses the question, Who is this generation of adults? and delivers the answers with no apologies. Michael Housholder in "Moving Out with Vision" describes how to begin the effort of reaching out. In "Sharing Good News" Pam Fickenscher lays out insightful principles for ministry that seeks to reach others with the message of God's transforming love. In "Worshiping in Spirit and Truth" Richard Webb energetically describes worship that engages hearts and minds. Mark A. Peterson in "Making Disciples" presents the realities and challenges to the church as we know it.

What next? God's mercy is new every day—let's get going and see what God has in store for us.

THE WHAT NEXT? PROJECT TEAM

introduction

God's

Janet M. Corpus

Janet lives in Philadelphia, Pennsylvania, and is a writer, pastor, and teacher. She has served congregations in Fairfield and Milpitas, California, and has worked in economic development and social policy.

ave reviews and sell-out audiences greeted the rock opera *Godspell* when it opened in May 1971. *Godspell* uses music, mime, and comedy to tell the story of Jesus' life and teaching according to Matthew's Gospel.

Nearly thirty years later, a new production of *Godspell* drew a capacity crowd at a church in downtown Philadelphia. Young people who were seeing the performance for the first time were enthusiastic about the show: "This is really good!" "I think the music's great!" They were also puzzled: "I don't get it." "Yeah, what's it about?"

Godspell debuted in 1971 to audiences who knew what the story was about, whether they were Christian or not. Their culture taught them enough about Jesus and his disciples that they understood the play. Not so today. Younger generations do not have that knowledge. They do not learn about Jesus at home nor do they learn about him in their environment.

Generation X, the demographic group born between 1964 and 1981, is the first widely unchurched generation in U.S. history. Tom Beaudoin, author of *Virtual Faith: The Irreverent Spiritual Quest of Generation X* (San Francisco: Jossey-Bass Publishers, 1998), describes his generation as serious spiritual seekers lacking in fundamental religious literacy. Churches, synagogues, and other religious institutions, he says, need to provide critical spiritual tools for this generation immersed in the images of popular culture. Beyond providing critical tools, the church has a mission to proclaim God's love to those who have not heard, many Gen Xers among them.

MESSAGE

As Christians we have amazing news to tell those who have never heard. "For God so loved the world that he gave his only Son, so that everyone who believes in him may not perish but may have eternal life. Indeed, God did not send the Son into the world to condemn the world, but in order that the world might be saved through him" (John 3:16-17).

God's love reaches out to embrace the world and to restore all people to eternal wholeness in the just and peaceful community for which God created us. This is our salvation. It is a gift we receive based not on our worthiness or merit but on God's grace. By the power of the Holy Spirit we are free to receive God's love and to live that love in our lives.

The message of God's love and gracious will for all people is an invitation to live with God and in community with God's people. Together we strengthen and encourage each other in discipleship. Members of the body of Christ, children of God, we are partners empowered by the Spirit for the work of love.

MISSION

God's love is expansive and embracing. So it is in the nature of the church as Christ's body in the world to spread the good news of God's love. Jesus' last words to his apostles were, "You will be my witnesses in Jerusalem, in all Judea and Samaria, and to the ends of the earth" (Acts 1:8). By these words Jesus outlined a mission strategy: Live and teach my love in your town, in your county and region, and in the world.

Global mission is familiar to churches in the United States and Canada. We are accustomed to sending missionaries around the world. In today's increasingly secular environment, domestic mission is becoming our highest priority. We are called to witness locally.

In domestic mission we face the same challenge as global missioners. How do we translate the gospel into local language for people who know little or nothing of Jesus Christ? How do we communicate the message of God's saving love? How do we do that in ways that embody love?

Domestic mission is a challenge because it means change. When we talk about "church" we are generally referring to what we are comfortable with—what makes sense to us and what we know. We are insiders. The church's mission is directed toward people who have not heard and for whom the church is not familiar because they are outside of it. Inviting them into community will change the community. We can anticipate that such change will enliven the church as new believers share new gifts in the body of Christ. Scripture and history teach and encourage us to meet the challenge of proclaiming the gospel to people different from ourselves.

DIVERSE MEDIA FOR A DIVERSE PEOPLE

God communicates in diverse ways. God came to Jacob in a dream (Genesis 28:12-15) and to Moses in a burning bush (Exodus 3–4). God spoke to Jesus from a cloud (Matthew 17:1-8). An angel messenger told Mary that she would bear a child (Luke 1:26-38). Saul heard Jesus' voice on the road to Damascus (Acts 9:1-19).

Teresa of Avila, mystic and activist in the 1500s, heard God speak as she read Augustine's writings in which he told of God's speaking to him in a garden. On Aldersgate Street, London, the eighteenth century church renewer John Wesley's heart was "strangely warmed" hearing Martin Luther's words on the book of

Romans. God spoke to preacher and civil rights activist Martin Luther King Jr. when he was alone in his kitchen late one night.

God has spoken in many and various ways to diverse people. The church's birth at Pentecost teaches us that diversity is an essential feature of the church. So we also must communicate in many and various ways.

At Pentecost (Acts 2:1-47) people from "every nation under heaven" (v. 5) were living in Jerusalem. Such diversity meant not only varied languages but also varied clothing, music, food, and smells. In their homelands the people knew different soils, plants, animals, and climates, all contributing to richly varied cultures.

Pentecost diversity goes even further. The Pentecost vision is inclusive across time. The Medes were present that day, a people who have long since disappeared from the earth. In his Pentecost sermon, Peter described both young and old as part of this vision.

Do we typically think of Pentecost as the celebration of a church diverse over time, an intergenerational church? The vision given to us at the birthday of the church challenges and encourages us in ministering to and with younger generations.

If we consider the myriad ways people have proclaimed and celebrated the good news of God's love, new possibilities for new generations do not seem so unusual.

Music: Tambourines (Exodus 15:20), trumpet, lute, and harp (Psalm 150:3), Gregorian chant, organ, guitar, jazz combo, African-American spirituals, rock.

Architecture: Stone cathedrals and store fronts. White clapboard buildings and tents. Living rooms and street corners. Pews and chairs around a kitchen table.

Clothing: Gold-trimmed vestments and street clothes. Suits and shorts. Patent leather and canvas. Belgian robes and flannel shirts.

Communications media: Letters, tracts, church bells, hotel room Bibles, newspaper ads, billboards, drums, radio shows, direct mail, televangelism, Web sites, hymnals, LCD projectors, song sheets.

The church has proclaimed God's love in Jesus Christ in widely varying ways. People determined to share the gospel have used what means were at hand and created new ones. Underlying our determination has been the freedom that comes from a message that is God-centered, not culture-centered. The message does not require a particular language. It does not center on one Bible passage or theological notion. It is not focused in one denomination or church practice.

THE MESSAGE IS GOD-CENTERED

The church can adapt because the church's message has an unchanging focus: the gospel of Jesus Christ who reveals God's love for all people and who, by the Holy Spirit, offers us eternal life and empowers us to live and serve in love.

The apostle Paul is our prime model of adaptability. A crucial dimension of his work as Christian evangelist was freedom to shape his proclamation to the cultural context in which he was speaking. "For though I am free with respect to all, I have made myself a slave to all, so that I might win more of them. . . . I have become all things to all people, that I might by all means save some. I do it all for the sake of the gospel, so that I may share in its blessings" (1 Corinthians 9:19-23).

Paul was free from all obligations except to proclaim the gospel of Christ's love for us. The law of love meant speaking in a way that incarnated the loving and inclusive embrace that he preached in Jesus Christ. Acknowledging diversity and division among the people with whom he worked, Paul subordinated his individual preferences for the sake of the gospel, going outside his "comfort zone."

Paul's context was different from ours. Yet it is the same in this respect: For many, the name of Jesus Christ is unknown. The church has not reached them with the good news of God's love. For new generations to hear the gospel, those who know Jesus Christ must make subordinate their cultural comfort to the task of sharing the gospel's blessings. This means more than acknowledging differences and it does not mean putting differences aside. It means accepting and embracing differences as positive vehicles for our proclamation.

Let's not misunderstand. Paul did not adapt his proclamation to cater to others, nor should we. Paul ministered "for the sake of the gospel" (v. 23). The criterion for adapting the message we bear is its focus on God. It centers neither on others' culture nor on ours, but on God.

JESUS CHRIST, MEDIUM AND MESSAGE

Jesus Christ is God's clearest, strongest message to us. In a particular time, place, and specific cultural setting, Jesus lived among us and spoke our language so that we could hear and understand. In Christ we see that to love means to make ourselves available for hearing, understanding, and speaking the language of the other person.

Anyone who has been in a setting where everyone was speaking an unfamiliar language knows how paralyzing that can be. We feel relief when someone addresses us in words we can comprehend. Then we are free to speak with the expectation of being understood. We can participate in conversation with the other person.

In Jesus Christ God speaks our language so that we can speak and respond with the knowledge that God understands us. Jesus comes to tell the truth of God's love toward us and God's will for our wholeness both now and eternally. In his incarnation Jesus is the medium of the good news he bears.

EACH ONE, THE MEDIUM

Like Jesus, each of us is a medium of the gospel message. While we cannot know each generation's culture any more than we can learn all the languages of the earth, we can be open and receptive. As we would respectfully welcome someone from a distant culture, imagine extending that cross-cultural grace to someone from another generation.

We can show God's grace in our presence, our prayers, and our openness to telling the story in a new way and singing God's praise to a different beat.

EVANGELISM IN POSTMODERN CULTURE

Even people who have never seen a *Stars Wars* movie will respond when you say, "May the force be with you." They can tell you who Darth Vader, C3PO, and Luke Skywalker are. You cannot expect the same level of recognition if you refer to the burning bush, Mary, or the Holy Spirit.

Today we minister in an environment in which people are not only unchurched; many Gen Xers have never been in a church and are without the most basic information about Christianity. How do we begin to communicate our faith when we are used to assuming that people have at least a vague idea of what we are saying before we say it?

Suspicious of organized religion and institutions in general, members of Generation X value authenticity and spontaneity over pat answers. Sharing basic Christianity will need to come through personal experience and relationships based on mutual acceptance.

For some it will come as a relief to know that proclaiming the gospel to younger generations means talking less and listening more. Listening is a simple and obvious strategy with people who are different from you, but listening between generations does not always come easily.

Consider this situation. In an adult class offered by a well-intentioned congregation, five young people talked about God, family, and friends; about the church's intolerance; and about the challenges of sharing their faith with others. They paused in their presentation for discussion. The older adults were eager to respond. They told stories from their youth intended to instruct the young people. They gave advice. They had answers. They asked no questions. Gradually, the older adults took over the conversation. Quietly one of the young adults packed up the compact disc she had brought to share in the final part of the session. Later she shrugged, "I'm not playing my music for them. They didn't listen to a word we said. They don't need me here."

A *Time* magazine article by Margot Hornblower reported on a 1996 survey that showed "72 percent of 18-to-24-year-olds believe this generation 'has an important voice, but no one seems to hear it'"(June 9, 1997). As technological and cultural changes increasingly segregate generations, the need to listen becomes more acute. Listening is an act of love and an embodiment of the very message we hope to share. Not only can listening help us understand the needs and longings of other generations, listening affirms the presence of a God who hears us all and is at work reconciling us together.

God is at work. Because someone has not heard the story of Jesus and his love does not mean she or he is beyond the reach of that love. One important role of an evangelist is to recognize God's presence and to give voice to that reality in the person's life. When we listen, we listen for God. We also listen for the other person who in speaking is revealed. We listen and in our listening receive that person as he or she is.

MAKING CHRIST KNOWN

Evangelism is in the nature of the church. Individually and together we reach out to share the good news of God's love revealed in Jesus Christ so that others may be drawn to new life with God and in community with God's people.

This proclamation in word and deed, our primary response to the love of God, infuses all that we do. Evangelism, worship, social ministry, education, pastoral care, property maintenance, and everything else bound up in congregational life can be a proclamation of the gospel. So also in the whole of our lives, our mission to proclaim the good news shapes what we do and how we do it.

Because evangelism involves all that we do, reaching out to Generation X can have profound and enlivening effects on the church. Christianity in our time and place is no longer "hand-me-down." For younger generations God is doing a new thing. The promise is not only of bringing the gospel to new generations but also of bringing new generations to the church and of deepening the spiritual life of those who already believe. ✠

a new generation

Christine L. Reifschneider

Christine lives in Colchester, Connecticut, is an undergraduate student in sociology, and is an active youth ministry leader at the local and regional level.

Author-date references for this chapter begin on page 38.

Katie never thought she would still be living at home at twenty-five. She figured she would find the perfect job after college, get her own apartment, and start her life. Katie majored in psychology with a minor in human resources. She wanted to work with children and make a difference. She found one job in a residential center for children with behavioral, emotional, and social difficulties, but it would have meant working the night shift. Her duties would have included feeding the residents dinner, bathing them, putting them to bed, and checking on them while they slept. The day jobs paid a little over minimum wage and she couldn't live on that.

IS THERE LIFE AFTER COLLEGE?

Not long ago, Katie saw a commencement address delivered by Bill Cosby. He asked the graduating class: "How many of you have taken any practical classes such as valet parking? 'Cause that's what most of you are going to be doing as a first job." She laughed, but she knew he was right. Her boyfriend graduated a year before her and couldn't find anything in his field either.

While in college Katie got experience in her field working in a day care center. She made seven dollars per hour, which is average for a college student. Things were okay there until the director left;

then the turnover in staff was constant. It was difficult to provide consistent care for the children when they were always looking at new faces. She often found herself alone with twelve preschoolers.

So after graduating and trying the "real world" for awhile, she went back to school. Now she is working on a graduate degree in career planning. She took a job as a nanny in the meantime.

Katie feels enthusiastic about her future. While looking for an internship for the summer, she came across just what she wanted—a job focusing on career planning, academic counseling, and administration. She thinks that employers will be looking for a broad base of experience.

Katie's experience is common among our generation. Gen Xers want to make a difference. We want to do something meaningful, but many of us can't support ourselves with jobs that match our skills, interests, and values. We feel lucky if we find a good-paying job at all.

Our generation is living its life in fast forward. We are trying to get ahead in a world full of one-way streets and dead ends. In our search for ourselves and for meaning in our lives, many of us feel a spiritual emptiness. We sense there's something more to life that we are missing. We are hungering for community. We are searching for God.

To begin to understand my generation, let's consider the various influences that have shaped Generation X and the other generations alive today.

DEMOGRAPHICS 101

Generation X. What does this term mean anyway? Douglas Coupland's novel *Generation X: Tales for an Accelerated Culture* is credited with coining the term (New York: St. Martin's Press, 1991). It is a general label that lends itself to many interpretations. The media's interpretation has been that the X stands for indifference. Our elders felt that as a generation we lacked motivation.

According to them, we thought that success should be handed to us on a silver platter and that we shouldn't have to work for it (Sacks 1998, 46). Our other labels have included Twenty-some-things, Thirty-somethings, Baby Busters, Postmoderns, Whiners, Slackers, and all the derivations of the word *slacker*. J. Walker Smith, coauthor of *Rocking the Ages* (Smith 1997), said in an interview, "It was Baby Boomers who latched onto the term Generation X. When Baby Boomers got to the end of the 1980s, their experience was completely different than their expectations about how life would unfold. All they really saw was a future they thought was going to be filled with contradictions, hardship, and reversals. . . . So the term X seemed to be exactly the sort of future they envisioned. . . . It was a Baby-Boomer projection of their disappointment onto the generation behind them" (Stoneman 1998, 46).

If there is one thing to know about this generation, it is that we do not like labels. To overgeneralize, lump all of us into a single category, and stick on a label is insulting. We embrace diversity and extreme individuality. Of all of the labels, Generation X seems to have the most staying power. So for the sake of clarity, in this book those of us born between 1964 and 1981 are referred to as Generation X.

What is the value of generalizing about a generation? Like people of my generation, perhaps you balk at being lumped together with Boomers, Silents, or Matures and take exception to the assertions about your generation. Sociologists have found that each generation has its own unique characteristics shaped by the national or worldwide events experienced during that generation's formative years. Knowing these general characteristics, even when they don't apply specifically to you as a Boomer or a Silent or to every Gen Xer you know, can give you a foundation for understanding and more effectively connecting with Generation X.

Of people living today, there are three generations that came before and one generation that arrived after Generation X. The World War II or GI Generation was born in or before year 1933.

They are the most politically savvy generation alive. They have been able to prepare and promote their own agenda. In *13th Gen*, authors Neil Howe and Bill Strauss describe them as "the best-insured, most leisured, and (in relation to the young) most afflu-ent generation of elders in American history" (Howe and Strauss 1993, 36). According to Howe and Strauss, Gen X sees this gener-ation as the engineers who constructed the societal institutions that in their heyday served a larger purpose. To Xers, the World War II Generation is a visionary age cohort that is at ease with progress. However, Xers also see this generation as "nonpartici-pants in cultural trends, irrelevant in values debates, and advocates of the sort of endless economic pump priming that threatens to bankrupt the future" (37).

The Silent, Swing, or Builder Generation was born between 1933 and 1945. They also have been shaped by the Depression and World War II. Howe and Strauss describe them as "the ones who refined and added nuance to what the GIs were doing." They grew up in a society that seemed excessively "conformist and they set about on a life mission of adding . . . other directedness and cultural pluralism. . . . They were the leading proponents of the civil rights movements [and] the nonviolent movements" (Lamb 1991). Most Silents "have the work ethic of their elders, believe in self-discipline and self-reliance, and hold traditional views of authority" (Dunn 1994).

The Silents, for the most part, raised Xers. For older Xers, Silents were Mom and Dad. For the younger Xers with Boomer parents, Silents still influenced their lives as psychiatrists, lawyers, community leaders, and school officials. According to Howe and Strauss, Silents were the adults most influenced by the self-fulfill-ment gurus of the 1960s and '70s. Some Silents saw their children as "roadblocks in the path of the midlife Silent quest to recapture a lost youth" (Howe and Strauss 1993, 40). As older Xers moved into young adulthood in the 1980s, Silent parents noted the differences between generations as demonstrated in behavior, acad-emic performance, and overall lifestyle, and were vocal about their disappointment.

Generation Y or the Millennials are those individuals born between 1981 and 2000. They were born at a time when society once again placed value on children. Some Xers have or will have children that fall into this generation. They have been born into a technological universe. They have much in common with Xers as far as family structure and cultural influences, but are described as more self-confident, less concerned about nuclear war, and raised with high expectations. This generation is still being defined, but Gerald Celente, author of *Trends 2000* (Warner Books 1997) says, "This new generation doesn't expect [to live the yuppie dream of making money]. This generation will lead a new renaissance in America" (Tasker 1997).

Then there are the Boomers. The Baby Boom generation was born into a prosperous post World War II America between 1946 and 1964. This was a time of suburbs, the nuclear family, rock 'n' roll, and television. Their growing-up years were marked by the Vietnam War and assassinations of key political leaders. The term "Generation Gap" was coined when Boomers hit their late teens and early twenties and rebelled against authority and society. Their suspicions of institutions and authority is an enduring attitude. Although a minority embraced the lifestyle, the generation is often characterized as a "free-loving hippie generation who dodged the draft, protested against the war in Vietnam, [and] attended Woodstock." (Williams and Coupland 1997, 27). The actions of a few shaped this generation to be highly suspicious of institutions and authority. Boomers made great strides in all of the movements of the time: women's, civil rights, black power, American Indian, environmental, anti-war, disabilities, and student movements to name a few. Generation X respects them for this.

Then something happened. The Boomers got older. According to Neil Howe, "During the 1970s . . . everyone expected the Boomers to become a great new political force. . . . By 1980 they became the yuppie, and they concentrated on a certain cultural perfectionism. Rather than involving themselves with politics, they detached themselves from institutional life, from having families, from having steady jobs." As they're moving into midlife, they're revealing more conservative morals as compared to their earlier years (Lamb 1991).

Boomers came of age at the time the first Xers were born. Now some of them are our parents and many are our bosses and teachers.

CASUALTIES OF GENERATION ME

The 1970s are notorious for many things. Bell-bottoms, disco, Watergate, the end of the Vietnam War, and the Brady Bunch are the staples of that decade. One thing the decade of the '70s was not known for was good parenting.

Generation X was born into an America that was not as accommodating to children as the previous generation had experienced—children of the Baby Boom were considered America's most precious commodity. For Generation X, it's not much of a leap to conclude we were a national burden. Times were a-changing. Overpopulation was an emerging concern and abortion rights a controversial Supreme Court case. According to the U.S. Public Health Service and Alan Guttmacher Institute, one out of every three fetuses was aborted in the 1970s (Howe and Strauss 1993, 56). In *Welcome to the Jungle*, Geoffrey Holtz writes about political leaders' response to these social issues. In 1970 the Nixon Administration formed the Commission on Population Growth to address concerns of overpopulation. The Commission concluded that any further population growth would be detrimental to America. It was "one of the major factors affecting the demand for resources and the deterioration of the environment in the United States" (Holtz 1995, 16). They predicted a grim economic future if the population was to keep growing. Holtz points out the irony that this study was conducted while the birthrate had been declining steadily since 1964.

At about the same time, organizations sprung up advocating childlessness for couples or that they have no more than one child. For the first time, the cost of raising a child was considered by society. People were wondering if that cost would be worth the sacrifices. Having children didn't become fashionable again until the early 1980s (Howe and Strauss 1993, 55).

Couples that did decide to have children were faced with discrimination and sometimes hostility. In major U.S. cities, landlords could legally turn a person away if he or she had children and they had the option of not renewing a lease if a woman tenant became pregnant. Holtz cites a 1979 study that showed seven out of ten apartment complexes in Los Angeles excluded children. In other cities such as Dallas, Houston, and Denver, seventy to ninety percent of new apartment complexes were adult-only (Holtz 1995, 10). Landlords were looking for single men and women or young professional couples that would pay a high price to not have to live near children. Families who could not afford their own homes had a difficult time finding a place to live and had to settle for older apartments in less desirable sections of town.

In the '70s parents increasingly turned to child-rearing experts for guidance. The psychologists of the time told parents to focus on themselves rather than on the child (Howe and Strauss 1993, 55). The prevailing thought was that the child would be fulfilled if the parents were fulfilled through career or divorce, for example. Personal sacrifices weren't necessary for their children's well-being. Holtz describes this thinking: Parents were told that children were perceptive. The child knew when something was wrong in a marriage, for example, and so divorce would not be a great shock. Further, parents were led to believe their children were resilient and would bounce back (Holtz 1995, 28). So moms and dads focused on themselves. They worked their way up the career ladder. If they felt that they would be happier divorced, then they got divorced. The children often felt left out of their own families.

With the Silent generation, the dissolution of marriage became acceptable for the first time in history. The divorce rate was soaring and the number of unwed mothers was on the rise. One-half of all Xers found themselves in single-parent homes at one point or another (Tapia 1994, 18). With divorce came the fear of abandonment, financial hardship, and sacrifice. Often in a divorce situation the kids were the last to know. They would wake up one morning and Daddy would be gone with no explanation. Mom may have worked part-time or not at all. Once divorced, she would have to work full-time. Joint custody and child support were not yet customary in divorce cases. It was assumed that Mom would get custody. Dad might stop by once in awhile, or not at all. Often, the only women who got child support were ones that knew how the system worked. They were usually educated and employed (Holtz 1995, 34-35). The women who had spent their time at a home with the kids could not get a well-paying job. They really needed the child support and did not know how to get it. Even in court-ordered support cases, there was no way to keep the father compliant. Often the checks would not come or would be much less than the promised amount. With or without child support, women made substantially less money than men. It was very hard for a mom to make mortgage payments and still supply all the basic necessities for herself and her kids. The house usually had to be sold (Howe and Strauss 1993, 60-61).

Other factors affected the childhood of Gen Xers. It seems that physical, verbal, and sexual abuse were on the increase in households. Geoffrey Holtz cites statistics from the American Humane Society showing that in one decade, from 1976 to 1985, the number of children victimized by child abuse grew by three hundred percent, from about one-half million to two million. Neil Postman, author of *The Disappearance of Childhood*, "hypothesized that because childhood innocence was no longer seen as a positive quality, and children were growing up more quickly, abusing them no longer seemed so appalling. . . . Children had become miniature adults, not innocents in need of protection" (Holtz 1995, 62).

Domestic abuse has been a silent epidemic plaguing this country. Family secrets are still considered sacred. Many of our generation who experienced abuse could not tell anyone what was happening out of the fear of repercussions. We suffered in silence.

THE ONE WITH THE MOST TOYS WINS

If there is a single song that characterizes the entire decade for Xers it is Madonna's "Material Girl." We spent the 1980s watching our parents obsess over money, success, power, and control. If our parents were still married or had remarried, the '80s brought financial security to most homes. Economically, the disappointment for the Boomers and the Xers did not set in until the downsizing of the late '80s (Stoneman 1998, 46). In the meantime, we were the wealthiest generation while in high school and college. Mom and Dad would give us money to do chores around the house that they did not have time to accomplish. We worked summer jobs and part-time jobs during the school year. Parents would often supplement this income with monetary gifts. It was like compensation for when they could not be home.

We were the latchkey kids. Our parents trusted us with the responsibility of being home alone, but felt we couldn't be trusted with the house key. We wore the key around our neck so that we wouldn't lose it. While home alone, we were not allowed to go outside or answer the phone or door. We were not allowed to play with our friends. When Mom and Dad got home after work, they were tired so we watched more television or played Pacman. Instead of learning from our parents and teachers, we were learning from the media. Bert and Ernie taught us to count. Kermit the Frog was our hero. Many of the other shows weren't so virtuous. The line between right and wrong was fuzzy and in some cases erased altogether.

The circumstances of our lives accelerated our maturity. We were not kids. We were little adults. We often became our single parents' best friend. They would talk to us about their boyfriends or girlfriends. They would talk to us about sex, love, and dating.

The boundaries between parents and children that had existed with older generations had disappeared. When our parents did remarry they seemed to forget they had children. We felt out of place in our new pieced-together families. We had step-parents and step-siblings. We had half-brothers and sisters who seemed to be more important than we were and it seemed we were always the ones getting into trouble. After all, we were the product of a failed marriage. Physically and emotionally, we were a generation alone.

When you leave a whole generation of children alone with a lot of money, what are they to do? When the going gets tough, the tough go shopping! Consumerism became our full-time job. We had to have the latest compact discs, video games, and clothes. We spent a considerable amount of time and money at the movie theater. When we were not consuming, we were at home playing with our new toys or watching MTV and planning our next trip to the mall. We worshiped popular culture.

Materialism masked our pain. We may have seemed happy— superficially we were. But underneath the material girl was a person who felt empty and alone. Some of us began experimenting with drugs, alcohol, and sexual activity at a very young age. We searched for anything that would numb the pain, or at least be a distraction from it. Maybe our parents did not know. Maybe they did and looked the other way. Some parents figured we were just repeating their youth of free love and marijuana. What they did not know is that we were dealing with AIDS and crack cocaine. The stakes had gotten much higher. By the time we reached high school we saw our friends move in and out of rehab clinics. Some tested positive for HIV. Some had attempted suicide. When we confided in our parents and counselors, we were not taken seriously—our lives looked fine from the outside. Adults couldn't understand what we were whining about.

For every generation there are events and ideologies that unite its members. For Xers it is a mosaic of popular culture. Our memories are marked with movies (*Star Wars*), songs ("Girls Just Wanna Have Fun"), music videos ("Thriller"), commercials (Where's the beef?), television shows ("Cheers"), board games

(Monopoly), sports (the WWF), fashion trends (parachute pants), body costuming (nose rings and spiked hair), and the Internet. Every Xer might attach a different event or significance to each piece of the culture. The odds are good though that each Xer will recognize a good number of the symbols that the media bombarded us with (Beaudoin 1998, 22-23).

On January 28, 1986, the *Challenger* space shuttle was launched with the first civilian on board, Christa McAuliffe. The shuttle never made it to space. It exploded. I was in fifth grade and had stayed home from school that day to watch the launch. Becoming an astronaut had been my goal. I was stunned. I watched the launch on the news over and over again and saw the debris come streaming down from the sky. I kept thinking that it wasn't real; it couldn't have happened and for months afterward I had nightmares. If there is one event that marked the life of every American Gen Xer this is it. Much like the Kennedy assassination for Boomers, we all know where we were and how we felt on that fateful day.

This is when we began to lose our sense of security and faith in institutions. Natural and human disasters showed us just how fragile life is.

WHATEVER

Our indifferent attitude, which many of our elders note, is a way for us to mask our anger and frustration about the world we live in. The very institutions and leaders that helped our parents and the generations before them are the things we don't trust. Too many of them haven't delivered what they have promised.

The consensus of older generations seems to be that Xers have had an inferior education and have been equipped with inferior skills. For those of us who worked while attending college to help pay tuition and who are still paying off student loans larger than our annual salary, this attitude is a harsh and discouraging reality (Howe and Strauss 1993, 70).

With the 1970s came the trend of open education. It was thought that the emphasis should be placed on self-esteem and how one felt rather than on the facts one knew. "From kindergarten to college, [scholastic] standards were allowed to weaken or disappear altogether" (74). Schools published handbooks stating student rights. There was less discipline—students were allowed to run their publications and clubs as they pleased. At the same time, rowdy students, meddling parents, divisive school boards, and strong opposition to school taxes were on the increase. Teachers had little support from anyone. They did whatever they could to survive from day to day (75).

As a result we learned what we were taught: journaling and how to be in touch with our feelings. We learned how to negotiate, how to be independent, and how to find information. We didn't learn math, science, or history. No matter what level of education we achieved, we were considered dumb (75-77).

The fact that we weren't united behind a social cause or in political activism is perhaps another reason our generation has been subject to negative stereotypes. According to a *National Review* article on Gen X voting, only 28 percent of 43 million American Xers are likely to vote compared with 68 percent of senior citizens. Forty percent of us identify ourselves as Independents, the rest are equally split between Democrats and Republicans (Fitzpatrick 1996, 46).

The lower voter turnout is tied to our skepticism of institutions and leaders. We don't believe that bureaucracy can accomplish anything. There is too much talk and too little action. The Nike slogan Just Do It! is our motto. There is little party loyalty mostly because there is little government loyalty. A survey by the civic group Third Millennium found that fifty-three percent of us believe that the soap opera "General Hospital" will outlast Medicare (Hornblower 1997, 62).

We have accepted the adage that if you want something done, you have to do it yourself. We see volunteerism as an alternative to politics. We are active in practical grassroots organizations. We can be found tutoring young children, working on houses, visiting the elderly, and serving meals to the homeless (Schaub 1998). A recent survey for Public Allies, a multicultural group supporting civic service found that Xers are public-spirited and that we are looking for new ways to connect with people and with the issues surrounding us (Gergen 1998, 68).

We want to make a difference.

THE NEW AMERICAN DREAM

The Gen Xer American Dream is different from what was previously termed "The American Dream." We don't want the 2.4 kids, 1.4 dogs, 2 cars and a house with a white picket fence. Suburbia may have worked for our grandparents, but it didn't work for our parents. We don't want to make the same mistakes they did.

If you are interested in learning about the Gen X mission in life, see the movie *The Matrix*. It is the story of a young office worker and computer hacker's search for the truth. The first dilemma occurs early in the movie when Neo has to decide if he wants to return to the normal routine of his illusions or if he wants to enter the world of reality in which there is no turning back. With little deliberation, Neo chooses to learn the truth.

Neo discovers that the world is not as it seems. It has been taken over by the Matrix. People have been turned into pawns of the system. They get up. They go to work. They come home. There is no individualism, no autonomy, no choice. The people cannot think for themselves and so they have no idea what has happened to them.

The Matrix is an Xer's worst nightmare and we wonder if we are already trapped in it. We saw our parents go to work every day. They worked long hours and spent the weekend catching up on the errands and chores not accomplished during the week. It was as if they were put on this earth just to work. They appear to have accepted this as their fate. But we believe there is more to life. Our parents live to work; we work to live. Our parents have stability with a few weeks off each year for adventure; we have adventure and take a few weeks off for stability. After all, we have to pay for our adventures somehow!

Our slacker stereotype is finally fading. Now that the economy is on the upswing, we have more employment opportunities. For most of the 1990s, entry-level positions within major corporations weren't available. Many of us worked at low-paying, even less gratifying, service industry "McJobs." We graduated from college and came back to our parents' houses because we couldn't afford to live on our own. While a person may be able to pay rent making six dollars an hour, she won't be able to eat as well.

The career component of the Xer American Dream is enhanced by an entrepreneurial attitude. Overall interest in corporate careers is at an all-time low. No one wants to put their time into a company sitting in a cubicle waiting for a big opportunity that may never come. Many post-secondary schools have added classes in entrepreneurialism. A University of Michigan study that concluded that 25- to 34-year-olds are trying to start their own businesses at three times the rate of 35- to 55-year-olds (Hornblower 1997, 62). We are our own bosses and becoming successful on our own and in our own ways. We certainly don't want to be chained to a desk for forty hours or more a week until we turn 65. We crave independence and autonomy. Xers want the flexibility to make our own schedules. We don't want to miss out on a personal or family life in lieu of a career.

We are intentional about our interpersonal relationships. We formed peer groups as children to act as pseudo-families. Gen Xers were easy prey for gangs and cults because we so badly wanted community we would take it in whatever form it was offered. Now, we still want community but we are skeptical. We don't take commitment on any level lightly.

Our idea of the American Dream may include some of the

usual things, but it certainly isn't limited to material objects. A 1996 *Swing* magazine poll found that thirty percent of us define personal success as a balance between work and home (Fitzpatrick 1996, 46). We also want what we haven't had: a family. We don't view wedding rings and children as status symbols, but as very serious commitments. Marriage is scary for us and so we are waiting until we are older to get married. Many of us see the same person much longer before we even consider marriage. For many of us, we cohabitate as a sort of trial run. Despite this, the divorce rate for couples in their twenties and thirties has remained the same (Hamilton et al 1998, 54). We know that there are obstacles to be overcome in any relationship and that our upbringing hasn't provided us with all the necessary tools. We don't go into marriage thinking we are going to live happily ever after, we go into marriage hoping it will last.

As parents, the Xer dream is to give our children the childhood we never had. That means as they grow we want to try to guard them from the harsh realities of life. We want to do everything we can to keep them from taking the same liberties that we took in our youth (Howe and Strauss 1993, 221). We want to teach them to scrutinize the messages handed to them by the media. We want to reinstate the boundaries that were erased during our adolescence. We want to give them a solid family experience, whatever the structure might look like. We know older generations wanted this for their children too, but we believe we have learned from their mistakes and will do things differently.

Xers are more accepting of diversity than older generations. Kevin Graham Ford in *Jesus for a New Generation* concludes that we are "less gender-specific than past generations," in fashion, hairstyles, careers, and sports (1995, 25). Despite the incidents of racial unrest highlighted on television and in newspapers, "we accept, respect, and socialize with each other much more than older Americans of differing backgrounds do, and this is a source of strength" (Holtz 1995, 207).

We don't just accept diversity, we expect it.

THE QUEST FOR THE TRUTH

In the movie, *The Truman Show*, Truman Burbank lives a simple, happy life. He has no idea that his whole world is an illusion. Truman was adopted by the Omnicam Corporation as an infant. Cristof, the creator of "The Truman Show," is a god, director, and father to Truman. Omnicam built a dome for Truman and his entire universe is encased inside of it. Every minute of his life has been filmed and broadcast around the world twenty-four hours a day. The people in his life are actors and actresses who come on the scene to play their parts in Truman's world and then go home to their own lives. Eventually, Truman realizes that too many unexplained events are occurring and he begins to question his surroundings.

Seemingly like Truman's world, our world is filled with artificial colors and flavors. We often wonder if we are trapped inside an inauthentic world, and one over which we have no control. Modernism provided us with a scientific base of knowledge about the world that is useful but incomplete. Discerning what is authentic and real in our world is difficult because we know even what appears to be reality can be manipulated. We are bombarded with information that is at best edited and at worst "hype." Ratings and sales drive many decisions in commercial media. Even information provided by "objective" journalists through news and network programming is influenced by corporate shareholders. Stories and people we see on television and in the movies are so carefully and perfectly presented they can never precisely represent the clumsiness and inaccuracies of living, breathing humans. Try as we might, we will never attain the flawlessness portrayed on screen.

Xers are tired of people putting on a show to try to sell us something. It doesn't matter if it's a faster modem, a new diet pill, or religion. If your product isn't organic, then don't bother. We are not interested.

What is the bottom line? We want the truth.

THE INFORMATION SUPERHIGHWAY

The phone book used to advertise "let your fingers do the walking" or "information at your fingertips." The directory was useful in its heyday, at which point we never could have imagined the Internet. Now information on anything a person could possibly conceptualize is just a mouse-click away. The accessibility of data is causing a digital divide between the information "haves" and the information "have-nots." If you are not surfing the Web, there is no way that you could possibly keep up with the ebb and flow of information. By the time a book or even a magazine is published and distributed, more recent research and information can be found on the Internet.

Gen Xers have grown up in the information age. We use the internet for everything: research, news, banking, shopping, stock trading, and relationships. The post office is becoming a piece of American history—who needs snail mail when you have e-mail?

Distance education is becoming the convenient way for adults to earn degrees and still balance their work and family life. Many of us take classes online. We can download the lectures in the middle of the night while wearing our pajamas! The Internet has become such a staple in the academic community that one college recently devoted two days to a "Cyber Survival Symposium." The college offered various workshops including "Internet Freedom: Anti-Censorship Arguments," "Legal and Ethical Issues: E-mail and Liability," and "Fortifying Your Computer for Personal Cyber Safety."

With the Internet, Xers take the good with the bad. There are many things out there we don't want to know about or see. As with everything else, if you don't like it, turn it off. We have always been a generation that enjoys instant gratification. The Internet satisfies this desire. It used to be that we would turn on the Weather Channel and within eight minutes we would get our local forecast. Now we go to our computers and just point and click and instantly it's there. One might think that with the convenience we would have more "free" time. Quite the opposite is happening. The Web is moving our lives at a quicker speed than ever. We are filling that free time with more tasks—instead of doing one task in ten minutes, we do three.

The Internet isn't going to go away, so all of us might as well use it to our advantage. By 2005, it is estimated that sixty percent of young adults will look to the Internet as the primary source for fulfilling their spiritual needs (Quintana 1999). Anyone hoping to be noticed by or to influence Xers needs to have a strong presence on the Web. Not having a home page is like having an unlisted phone number.

RELIGION VERSUS SPIRITUALITY

For me, the most intriguing part of the movie *The Matrix* occurs when Neo goes before the Oracle to find out if he is the one who can save the world from the illusions imposed by the Matrix. As Neo enters the Oracle's kitchen, she says to him, "Don't worry about the vase." Neo responds with "What vase?" and accidentally knocks it to the ground. The Oracle asks Neo, "Would you have knocked over the vase if I didn't tell you that you were going to?" In other words, what determines our future? Are the actions we take and the random circumstances of our experience the only things that determine our future? Or is there something more? Perhaps some higher order?

The questions raised by the Oracle are typical of the questions Gen Xers have been asking. They are questions about our niche in society, fate, the meaning of life, and God, and they regularly show up in movies, music, and on the Internet. Gen Xers are exploring spirituality in all different facets of our society. In pop music culture a few examples include Jewel's latest CD "Spirit" where she states "We are in God's hands." Sarah McLaughlin sings "You're in the arms of the angels." And NSYNC serenades us with "God must've spent a little more time on you." As Tom Beaudoin states in *Virtual Faith*, this is a generation that has no problem searching for God through the context of popular culture. God is not contained within the four walls of the church. For Xers, God is everywhere.

Most Xers believe in something that represents a higher power in their lives, but it may not be God as traditionally understood in Western religion. In fact Xers are not at all sure what "God" really is. For this reason, you will not find many Xers in church. More likely, you will find them at a bookstore browsing through the New Age section. They have many questions and are searching for a forum for spiritual exploration in which no question is stupid and no answer is too basic. Xers are searching for a place where they can share their ideas with each other. They are searching for community.

Many church members think that young adults are missing because we have not settled down with a job, spouse, and family. They still believe that Xers will come to church when we have children. We don't. Many of us were not brought up with a strong religious connection. We may want our kids to have morals and values consistent with the Ten Commandments and the Golden Rule, but we find other ways of providing these. We use movies from the media. Christian education has been reduced to animated Noah's Ark videos. Again, the media becomes our spiritual connection. The problem is that it is apart from community and accountability.

But this is good news for Christian congregations. God calls the church to be a community where people can meet Jesus Christ in the midst of all their doubts and questions. As the church we have an opportunity to put a Bible in people's hands, to share the love of Jesus with those who have worn a cross all their lives and yet do not know who it is who hung on that cross.

Already throughout North America, Xers are coming to know Christ's love through the ministries of honest and healthy churches. In many cases we are finding that our values resonate with Jesus' values. However, unchurched young adults present a challenge to congregations. Gen Xers are skeptical of proselytizing religions and institutions that promote their way is the "only right way." The postmodern mind will probably not believe that Christian truth is the absolute truth or the only truth. Don't expect us to affirm immediately the story of Jesus as the only story. For our generation, Christianity is only one of many religious perspectives. So, initially don't expect us to see it as any more or less valid than any other perspective. We have been exposed to many and varied cultures and world views, and we are suspicious of anyone who says, "We are right and you are wrong."

Gen Xers are also suspicious of religious people whose behavior seems to contradict the ideals they supposedly uphold. For us it is difficult to take seriously a church where the leaders seem to be unable to practice what they preach. For example, we wonder why so many priests and pastors have been brought up on charges of sexual misconduct. On the other hand, we are not inclined to trust congregations full of "perfect" people. We are looking for religious communities where people are real. We are looking for honesty. Gen Xers are looking for communities of faith where people struggle over issues that affect their lives.

WHAT'S A CHURCH TO DO?

A common myth is that our churches have no young adults. If you look around your congregation you will probably find a few. This is the group of people to start with. For Xers that are already involved in your congregation, include them as planners and leaders of your worship service. Provide programming and Bible studies geared specifically to them. To keep them involved through their college years and beyond, there needs to be a place for them.

Service projects are often an effective way for seekers to enter the community of faith and a ministry through which existing members can "make a difference." Xers are just as apt to discover God at work in soup kitchens, homeless shelters, hospitals, and on the streets, as they are in candle-lit sanctuaries.

Doug Pagitt, formerly of the Leadership Network in Dallas, Texas, offers some innovative ideas. He suggests that a church trying to reach this generation should find someone, paid staff or a volunteer, who fits this demographic, someone who would understand the needs of Xers. With this person, the congregation could create a worship experience specifically for the target audience.

You might need to create an independent name and personality for this kind of ministry. Sponsoring service projects such as Habitat for Humanity will give your church exposure in a realm where these young adults want to participate. Another idea is to start a reading group in your local bookstore-café or another environment this generation is comfortable in. The discussion could be on a particular book of the Bible or a popular book that ties in with the beliefs of the church. This discussion could be a springboard to an invitation to your congregation. You might also host community-wide workshops on topics that Gen-Xers are interested in such as job improvement, parenting, and spirituality, to name a few.

In some ways the church overestimates what it takes to do ministry with Generation X. You need to listen and be open to change. Be authentic with people. Be real. Be honest. Admit brokenness and practice what you preach. As you do this, you will find that your ministry will connect not only with my generation but with people of all ages. Our spiritual hunger is real.

The chapters that follow offer practical insights into ministry with Generation X. Each context is different, each situation is unique, but there are some common themes and principles about ministry that connects. ☧

REFERENCES

Anderson, Kerby. "Truth Telling to a Truth Denying Generation." *The Dallas/Fort Worth Heritage*, January 1997. www.fni.com/heritage/jan97/Kerby.html

Beaudoin, Tom. *Virtual Faith: The Irreverent Quest of Generation X*. San Francisco: Jossey-Bass, 1998.

Brians, Paul. "Reason, Romanticism & Revolution" course materials. Washington State University, Mar. 11, 1998. www.wsu.edu/~brians/hum_303/enlightenment.html

Buck, William R. and Tracey C. Rembert. "Just Doing It!" *E Magazine: The Environmental Magazine*, Sep./Oct. 1997, Vol. 8, Issue 5.

Coupland, Douglas. *Generation X: Tales for an Accelerated Culture*. New York: St. Martin's Press, 1991.

Dunn, William. "The Eisenhower Generation." *American Demographics*, July 1994.

Fields, D. Martin. "Postmodernism." *Premise*, Vol. II, No. 8, September 27, 1996. www.capo.org/premise/95/sep/p950805.htm

Fitzpatrick, Kellyanne. "The X Files." *National Review*, Nov. 11, 1996, Vol. 48, No. 21.

Gergen, David. "The Nation's New Patriots." *U.S. News and World Report*, Nov. 2, 1998, Vol. 125, Issue 17.

Gott, Richard. "The Origins of Postmodernity." *New Statesman*, Feb. 26, 1999, Vol. 129, Issue 4425.

Graham Ford, Kevin. *Jesus for a New Generation*. Downers Grove, Ill.: InterVarsity Press, 1995.

Hagevik, Sonia. "From Ozzie and Harriet to the Simpsons: Generations in the Workplace." *Journal of Environmental Health*, May 1999, Vol. 61.

Hamilton, Kendall, Pat Wingert, et al. "Down the Aisle." *Newsweek*, July 20, 1998, Vol. 132, Issue 3.

Holtz, Geoffrey. *Welcome to the Jungle.* New York: St. Martin's Press, 1995.

Howe, Neil and Bill Strauss. *13th Gen: Abort, Retry, Ignore, Fail?.* New York, Random House, 1993.

Hornblower, Margot. "Great Xpectations." *Time,* June 9, 1997.

Klages, Mary. "Modern Critical Thought, Lecture Notes, Postmodernism," Dec. 3, 1997, University of Colorado at Boulder. www.colorado.edu/English/ENGL2012Klages /pomo.html

Mizrach, Steve. "Modern Primitives: The Accelerating Collision of Past and Future in the Postmodern Era." *Perforations,* Oct. 26, 1997. noel.pd.org/topos/perforations/perf6/ modernprimitives.html

Quintana, Desiree. Presentation, ELCA Summit on Youth. Atlanta, Ga., Feb 7, 1999.

Sacks, Peter. "No . . . Generation X Is Not OK." *American Enterprise,* Jan./Feb. 1998, Vol. 9, Issue 1.

Schaub, Diana. "Gen X Is OK." *American Enterprise,* Jan./Feb. 1998, Vol. 9, Issue 1.

Slaughter, Michael, ed. *Out on the Edge.* Nashville: Abingdon Press, 1998.

Smith, J. Walker, *Rocking the Ages.* New York: HarperBusiness, 1997.

Strauss, William, and Neil Howe. Interview by Brian Lamb. *Booknotes.* C-SPAN, April 14, 1991. www.booknotes.org/transcripts/10114.htm

Stoneman, Bill. "Beyond Rocking the Ages." *American Demographics,* May 1998.

Svensson, Albert. Communication and Social Change. University College of Cape Breton, March 3, 1997. http://w1.303.telia.com/~u30303295/UCCB/ terms355.html

Tapia, Andres. "Reaching the first post-Christian generation." *Christianity Today*, Sept. 12, 1994, Vol. 38, Issue 10.

Tasker, Fred. "Here Come the Millennials: With a New Generation Coming of Age, a New Set of Attitudes Is on Its Way." *The Seattle Times*, July 31, 1997.

Wagner, Cynthia G. "Generational Shifts in Values." *Futurist*, Mar. 1999, Vol. 33, Issue 3.

Williams, Angie and Justine Coupland. "Talking About Generation X: Defining Them As They Define. . . ." *Journal of Language and Social Psychology*, Sep. 97, Vol. 16, Issue 3.

moving out with VISION

Michael Housholder

Michael serves as pastor of Lutheran Church of Hope, West Des Moines, Iowa.
The congregation was organized in 1994 and has grown
to an average worship attendance of 1,350 people.

A spirit of genuine enthusiasm blew through Lutheran Church of Hope in West Des Moines, Iowa, on a warm Saturday afternoon. Everything seemed so right: bright sunshine, a cool breeze, and the sounds of music in the air—live outdoor rock 'n' roll mixed with the voices of people praising God on picnic blankets. As worship ended, spontaneous hugs broke out with reckless abandon, at least for Iowa Lutherans! It was a final exclamation point at the end of a practically perfect day.

A HOPE STORY

Lutheran Church of Hope had invited the community to come and get a "Taste of Hope," and the people did come. By the mini-van loads, they poured into the parking lot and onto the front lawn for an afternoon of getting acquainted with a new church. Mission accomplished, or so it seemed.

Then came Kelly. Almost everyone else left with at least two things that day: a smile and a packet of information about the church. But not Kelly. Kelly left with neither and did not return to the church for more than a year. A college graduate, twenty-five years old, financially secure, and popular (though not entirely satisfied with career or peers), Kelly had not been inside a church building since fourth grade Sunday school. Over the years, she had openly questioned the need for organized religion in her quest to be spiritually satisfied. She was searching for life, but certainly was not expecting to find it in a church. As she left the "Taste of Hope" celebration, I invited Kelly to come again.

"Thanks. I might do that." Kelly said. "Which one of your services do people my age attend?"

My inadequate answer to Kelly's simple question started slowly, hit an awkward pause, and then just died, because there was no answer!

Pre-Kelly hope

Lutheran Church of Hope was a rapidly growing new church bursting with excitement. The church grew out of a desire to build a Christ-centered and mission-minded ministry—a church built on the rock of faith and the marching orders of Jesus: "Go therefore and make disciples of all nations, baptizing . . . and teaching" (Matthew 28:19-20).

With passion and energy, the church embraced Jesus' Great Commission, but before Kelly no one really paid much attention to demographic detail. Kelly's question led the church to an interesting discovery: the overwhelming majority of the members consisted of young Baby Boomers and their children. At the same time, the neighborhoods surrounding Hope included both young Boomer families and a lot of young adults like Kelly (Generation X), but hardly anyone Kelly's age attended Hope.

Kelly was invited to Hope because a friend wanted God to change her life and thought Hope might be the place, but God is full of surprises! God used Kelly to change the church first, and then the church to change Kelly!

Post-Kelly hope

Lutheran Church of Hope was missing a generation and hardly anyone noticed. Then came Kelly and her simple question that served as a wake-up call and a defining moment for the church. Within three months of Kelly's first visit, the changes at Hope started to show. Saturday worship became more Generation X "friendly." While not a dedicated service for one generation, as some churches do with great effectiveness, the preaching and music was planned with people like Kelly in mind: casual, come-as-you-are atmosphere, "unplugged" guitars, creative percussion, original lyrics, and Generation X worship leaders. The entire feel of the service changed. Somewhat surprisingly, a lot of the young Boomers continued to worship at this service despite the Generation X makeover, demonstrating perhaps that the permanent-ink, dark black lines so often drawn between generations really ought to be sketched with a much lighter pencil and a whole lot more gray. One year later, and just in time for Kelly's second visit to Hope, the majority of those who attended Hope's Saturday service were in their twenties, and overall attendance was way up.

Additionally, by the time Kelly returned to Hope, a number of healthy Generation X small groups had been established. A commitment had also been made to encourage Kelly and others of her generation to take on a variety of key leadership roles in the church. This blend of generation-based small groups and intergenerational church leadership helped to produce a climate of unified diversity at Hope. More important, it allowed one church in one community to carry out more faithfully Jesus' Great Commission.

Your story

This, of course, is just one church's story.

Every church is unique. The context of your story and your church may be similar to Lutheran Church of Hope in some ways and vastly different in others—and this is worth noting. One of the greatest temptations for church leaders today is modeling our ministry on the contextual details of another ministry. This approach all too often results in disappointment and disaster. Do not go there! Instead, like a wise prospector panning for gold, try to discern and separate the contextual details (fool's gold) from the universally transferable principles (pure gold). Cash in the good stuff and throw the rest away.

What is your story? What are the transferable principles in Hope's story for you? How can you lead a church to develop a ministry to Generation X that is both faithful to Christian mission and life-giving to those you are trying to reach?

To answer these questions, first take a closer look at your congregation. Second, dare to dream—ask for God's vision to be revealed to you regarding what your church's ministry to Generation X should be. Third, make the dream come true—once you receive a vision to reach Generation X with the gospel of Jesus Christ, make the move from concept to reality, and from articulating your ministry to actually doing your ministry. Fourth, celebrate the ministry, and after the celebration start all over again and dream bigger next time!

But one step at a time.

STEP 1: TAKE A LOOK AT YOUR BODY

How's your body?

Go ahead. Take a close look—at your congregation. Who do you see? Who greets you at the door on Sunday morning? Who hands you a bulletin? Who leads the music? Who runs the sound system? Who serves communion? Who preaches? Who sits next to you? Who talks to you after the service? Is something missing? Or, more to the point, is someone missing?

The apostle Paul writes, "Now you are the body of Christ and individually members of it" (I Corinthians 12:27). In the same chapter, Paul notes that "the eye cannot say to the hand, 'I have no need of you,' nor again the head to the feet, 'I have no need of you'" (v. 21).

The church body has need for all parts to be active in order to

44

be whole. Yet, if we take an honest look at many of our congregations, we will discover that we are missing some very important parts. Generation X is, generally speaking, missing in action! Some never came to church. Some are drifting away, concluding that the church is obsolete and irrelevant, and choosing to search for the way, the truth, and the life in all sorts of counterfeit places. They stand apart, disconnected from the rest of the body, and that is not healthy for either the generation or the church.

Time to 'fess up!

What can the church do? We can start by avoiding the temptation to take a finger-pointing, self-righteous stand—like the Pharisee's "holier-than-thou" prayers in the temple (Luke 18:9-14)—when in fact we have much to confess. True, many in Generation X are moving away from the church for reasons as old as original sin: a preference for relativism rather embracing any of God's absolutes; a self-defeating effort to create God in their own image; to be the potter instead of the clay; to be as God rather than of God.

Yet it is also true that many in today's church have over-labeled and under-estimated Generation X—and it is on this point that our confession of sin begins. Generation X is not a group of Slackers or Boomer wannabes. They have their own culture of music, art, and worldview. And contrary to what older generations may think, they have no plans to give it up. Church leaders who are Boomers or Builders must let go of the condescending attitude toward Generation X that says, "When you grow up you will be just like us." Generation X will not just eventually grow up, show up, and automatically fall in love with the form, structure, and style of Boomer or Builder-led churches.

High stakes

Reaching Generation X is not a simple task. It is not enough to just sit back and wait. It demands more from leaders and goes much deeper than just making a few stylistic changes. Throwing some new contemporary worship hymnals in the pews or using a

Generation X sermon illustration every once in a while will not solve the problem of our missing body parts.

What will work? The church needs to talk less and listen more, label less and love more. If we never learn to listen and love, how can we hope to gain trust? If we do not gain trust, how can we hope to communicate the gospel? If we do not communicate the gospel, where is the hope?

The stakes are high. Today's church is not as strong as we could be, not as whole as we should be. Tomorrow's church depends on reaching new generations today. Reaching Generation X, then, is about the survival of the church and the collective soul of a generation dying to find life.

With so much at stake, the time has come for the church to move, but before we get up and go, let us be humble and wise enough to ask God for directions.

STEP 2: DARE TO DREAM

Once a congregation develops a passion for reaching Generation X, the next step is to find a clear, God-breathed vision (what God calls you to be) to carry out the task.

Vision has become a bit of an overused buzzword over the past decade, used to define almost everything from business plans to personal goals to the dreams of a politician for a nation. But the vision thing was not invented by modern culture.

God-breathed visions have been around as long as people have been around:

God to the first human beings: Be fruitful and multiply! (Genesis 1:28)

God to Noah: Build an ark! (Genesis 6:14-21)

God to Abraham and Sarah: Have a baby so I can start a great nation through you, even though you are both pushing

100! (Genesis 17:1-21)

God to Moses via a burning bush: Get my people out of Egypt! (Exodus 3:1-12)

Why dream?

In all of these biblical examples, not only are clear visions from God very much the norm, they are also bigger than life. In other words, God's real life plans for us are often much bigger than our wildest worldly dreams.

Apply this truth to the church's complex challenge of reaching Generation X, and suddenly there comes the realization that with a God-breathed vision, there is hope! Efforts to bring Generation X into the church seem implausible until we remember we are not alone—God is with us "always" (Matthew 28:20) and with God nothing is impossible (Luke 1:37). The presence of a God-breathed vision, then, provides powerful inspiration and the courage to dream without worldly limits. A clear vision from God also helps church leaders to "see" where we are going. This is vitally important. A church with passion, gifts, and desire but no vision will wander aimlessly, like a gifted marathon runner who loses sight of her goal—to stay on course and cross the finish line first. Paul encourages the church to "run in such a way that you may win" (1 Corinthians 9:24).

A God-breathed vision for reaching Generation X will include specific answers to important questions: "Which way should we run?" "What is the goal?" "What will the results of this ministry be when we cross the finish line?"

The vision God provides may be shocking at first, in terms of magnitude. The goals may appear to be impossible to reach. But do not let the vision intimidate you. Remember, these visions and dreams contain God's plan for your life and your ministry. Trust God! Dare to dream!

How to dream?

How do you catch a God-breathed vision? How do you discover God's dream for you and your church? Get seriously involved in some good conversation: first with your trusted God (pray for vision) and then with some trusted friends (test the vision).

Pray. One of the greatest temptations for passionate church leaders is failing to make a distinction between God's vision for ministry and our own. Instead of searching for God's vision, we cast our own and try to drag God along for the ride! When you dance with God, who leads? Many good-looking visions for reaching Generation X end in failure not because the ministry was poorly planned or because the people leading the ministry were not adequately talented, but because the vision did not come from God.

To avoid this futility, pray! Engage in an ongoing prayerful conversation with God. The purpose of this conversation, which necessarily must be two-way (talk and listen) is not to talk God into your latest dream, but to ask God to reveal a new dream for your ministry.

So listen. Turn down the volume of your own prayerful voice. Open your ears. God can speak to you through the Bible, through the proclamation of the gospel, through the sacraments, and through the Holy Spirit in a variety of ways and settings. Biblical examples teach us that for Jacob, it was a dream (Genesis 28:12-15); for Moses, it was a burning bush (Exodus 3–4); for Saul, it started with the voice of Jesus on the road to Damascus (Acts 9:1-19). Perhaps you will hear the voice of God. Perhaps the Holy Spirit will plant an equally clear but nonverbal vision at the very depth of your soul. Or perhaps for you it will be more like a burning heart than a burning bush—a soft but consistent tug from the Holy Spirit.

If the call to fulfill a vision truly comes from God, you will not be able to ignore it. God has a reputation for persistence. Moses was initially very reluctant to accept God's vision, and tried over and over again to change God's mind: "O my Lord, please send someone else" (Exodus 4:13). But God would not be denied.

God does not create people without a purpose. If God has already given you a vision, accept it with faith—no matter how intimidating—and prepare for action. If you are uncertain, concentrate less on telling God about your dreams and more on listening to God's plans. It is easier to hear God when our ears are open and our mouths closed.

Test. After you come to the place in your conversation with God where you begin to feel confident of a vision for reaching Generation X, it is time to start a few more conversations with trusted friends for the purpose of testing the vision.

When Moses finally accepted God's vision, he immediately engaged in conversations with others regarding what he believed God was calling him to do: his father-in-law Jethro, his brother Aaron. Then Moses met with the entire assembly of the Israelite elders (Exodus 4:18-31). None of them voiced any disapproval, and the elders became so inspired by God's vision for Moses, "they bowed down and worshiped" (Exodus 4:31).

Following the example of Moses provides at least two major benefits for church leaders today.

First, testing a vision you believe to be from God with trusted friends will help provide additional affirmation or challenge you to deeper soul-searching. Either way, you will be strengthened for the journey.

Second, when you test God's vision in conversation with others, you automatically begin to share the ministry. James Lindberg, a pastor at Hosanna Lutheran Church in Lakeville, Minnesota, is responsible for leading the church's ministry with Generation X. Lindberg has experienced the benefits of intentionally sharing his visions with a team of volunteer leaders before attempting to turn the dreams into ministry realities. He explains, "After I share the vision, I encourage the volunteer leaders either to accept it or hammer it beyond recognition, because they are the ones who are going to make it happen. The process is open, and that allows the church members to take on more ownership of the vision and therefore the ministry."

It works—Hosanna is ministering effectively to Generation X, and developing a solid base of young adult leaders at the same time. Sharing vision helps to build a team, which in turn helps to build effectiveness and momentum for actually making ministry happen.

STEP 3: MAKE THE DREAM COME TRUE

This is the most important, and sadly the most neglected, step in the church's effort to reach Generation X. Lots of well-meaning congregations with good intentions have great God-breathed visions, but nothing really happens. In the church today, we are better at dreaming dreams than making them come true. So how can we change and improve? How can we get moving? What needs to happen for a church to move from a God-breathed and beautiful vision to real-world, life-changing ministry?

Start by identifying "dream killers"—things that keep a good vision from turning into a good ministry. Once you know the dream killers, then focus on the dream builders.

All talk, no action

Imagine, for the sake of illustration (and a little fun) that the Star Trek starship *Enterprise* is real and you have been invited to be a part of the original crew. For many years, detailed preparations are made. The spaceship is designed and constructed, you and the rest of the crew receive intensive training, and a mission statement is drafted: "Boldly go where no one has gone before!" Finally, the launch day arrives. You settle into your station right next to Mr. Spock, and observe that all systems are go for launch. Just then, Captain Kirk barks out the first and only order of the day: "Mr. Sulu, let's just park this thing and go home!" That would be absurd! Why go to all the trouble of putting together a spaceship, crew, and mission statement to "go" and then just "park it"?

It is absurd, yet that is what can and does happen in the church. We ask for and receive a vision from God, plan and prepare for the fulfillment of that vision with countless meetings, and then— when the time comes to launch the ministry—no one pushes the "blast off" button and the vision dies.

Specifically regarding Generation X, many church leaders have done some hard work learning the vocabulary. Many have even become fluent in discussing generation-based issues in the church and are able to make subtle distinctions between Builders, Baby Boomers, Generation X and Y. But talking about generations fluently is not an adequate substitute for ministering to generations faithfully.

Ministry, by definition, is something people do, or it is not really ministry. All of our talk can be quite impressive at first, but if talk does not lead to action, it is little more than vanity.

Fear of failure

What if it you try to reach Generation X and it does not work? Welcome to the club. Jesus was rejected by many of his followers who left the ministry because his teaching was too hard (John 6:60-68). On the day of Pentecost, about 3000 were baptized, but others rejected the message and claimed the apostles were drunk (Acts 2:13,41). Failure in the church needs to be redefined from "not meeting all of our objectives" to "not trying." Do not give up.

Over-analysis

If you dissect a frog, do not expect the pond-hopper to live. Avoid the temptation to over-analyze a vision. Some things will not be learned about a ministry until the ministry begins.

Ryan Surber received a God-breathed vision to start a concert ministry and Christian nightclub for young Gen Xers in Iowa. Surber established a board, built teams of volunteers, and then made an important move for the development of the ministry even though some thought it was "too early"—he actually did a concert. He booked several bands who, because of their style and reputation, would reach an audience of at least 750. Only two hundred people showed up. The next concert, Surber planned for 350, and eight hundred people showed up! What did he learn from the experience? "Lots. I learned that we can not label Generation X, or put Gen Xers in a box, musically. Just when I thought I knew what kind of music my generation wants, I was surprised." Surber knew as much as anyone about Generation X and Christian contemporary music when he started, but now he knows more. Actual ministry experience is a great teacher.

Build a team

Do not try to move from vision to ministry by yourself. Lone Ranger ministries rarely happen—and, in fact, even the Lone Ranger had a partner to share the work! Build a strong and positive team to do Generation X ministry, not a committee to talk about Generation X. It is better to have ten people who have a passion for reaching Generation X that leads to action than one hundred people who want to look into the possibility of starting a Generation X ministry. Review the strategic ministry planning on pages 55–58 and adapt them to suit your purposes.

Coordinate the team

Activate as much of the congregation as possible, not just those who already fit the Generation X demographic. Pay close attention to spiritual gifts and place people in roles accordingly. Let the prayer chain pray for the ministry. Let the gifted organizers organize. Let the singers sing and the drummers drum. Most important, seek out gifted young adult small-group leaders for the purpose of building healthy Christ-centered relationships within the church.

Balance accountability and freedom

If you are starting a new ministry to Generation X and it grows, the possibility of a church developing within a church becomes real. Because of this, some leaders might fear that targeting a specific age-group of people like Generation X is a threat to the unity of a congregation. It is.

Still, if a healthy balance between accountability and freedom is provided and well communicated, needless conflicts and power struggles can be avoided. Particularly in the early stages of a new generation-based ministry, a church leader must be willing and able to communicate the vision—effectively and repeatedly. In doing this, the congregation will be reminded over and over again the purpose and goal of a new ministry within the congregation. Each time the vision is communicated, congregation members are given an opportunity to make it their own.

This often overlooked step is key to maintaining the peace and providing for additional healthy growth for any new generation-based ministry.

Provide climate control

Effective church leaders provide adequate "climate control" for any new ministry. This involves a regular recasting of the vision for the sake of the ministry, addressing questions before they become complaints, like "Why is our church putting so many resources into a ministry to Generation X?"

Leadership support

Leaders need support—prayer, appreciation, education, care, and love. In developing a ministry for the sake of reaching Generation X, the potential for failure (as the world defines it) and burnout is high. Take care of the leaders and they will take care of the ministry.

STEP 4: CELEBRATE—AND DREAM SOME MORE

If the vision of reaching Generation X is realized, stop and celebrate! Give God all the glory! Far too often, we are tempted to hurry into the next challenge before we take any time to celebrate the current victory.

Recently, during a service at Lutheran Church of Hope, a previously unchurched young man stood up to tell his story of faith. For years, he had been lost in a world of drug abuse and sexual addiction. He was well known in the community and most of the congregation knew most of his story. He started his testimony by smiling and looking out around the congregation for almost a full minute. Then he shouted out, "I love Jesus!" The congregation laughed and then started to cheer, spontaneously! They were taking time to celebrate and praise God for bringing this man to a new life through faith in Jesus Christ. As he continued to tell his story, people continued to laugh, and cry, and applaud. When he finished, the congregation enjoyed a time of Christ-centered fellowship and more celebration.

Every church has stories to tell and victories to celebrate. Never underestimate the power of a good party in your church! A Holy Spirit-inspired celebration not only provides a good mark for a church to say "this happened and we are overjoyed," it also serves as a renewing agent for the sake of future ministry challenges—another thing that every church has in common.

When the celebration has happened, then start dreaming again. Go back to "Step 1" and ask God "What next?" May God give you a great dream to reach Generation X, then may all your dreams that come from God come true. ✚

STRATEGIC MINISTRY PLANNING

The following worksheets have been adapted from Strategic Ministry Planning Guide, © *1998 Evangelical Lutheran Church in America. Used by permission.*

Bringing together your leadership team

1. List the members of your planning team.

2. What gifts does each member bring to the team?

3. What is each team member's area of responsibility?

Planning team process

1. Close listening. Gather the planning team and make arrangements to listen in the following ways:

- Conduct interviews with people in their twenties and thirties.

- Gather and listen to music albums and videos that are popular among this generation.

- Gather and review demographic information on your community and this generation in your community.

2. Read about Generation X and postmodern culture.

3. Build a solid spiritual foundation. Hold a one-day retreat focused on Bible study and prayer.

4. Draft a strategic ministry plan.

INTERVIEWS WITH GENERATION X

As part of the listening process, bring together one or more small groups of people in their twenties and thirties for conversation. Think about gathering in an informal setting and a place where the group would feel comfortable.

Ask the following questions of the group or use them to help you shape conversation topics. After the conversation(s), record their responses (see #1-3 below).

• What do you think is the most pressing need for people right now?

• How do you think those needs can be met?

• What's your favorite kind of music? What makes it your favorite?

• What disturbs you and your friends the most about American culture?

• What do you think of most religions?

• Why do you think most people don't attend church?

• If you were to look for a church, what kind of things would you look for?

• What advice would you give to a minister who really wants to be helpful to people in your generation?

1. With one or two short sentences, summarize the responses to the questions you asked.

2. What are some of the central themes reflected in the lyrics and music that your planning team listened to?

3. How will what you have learned from these two activities impact your ministry strategy?

REVIEWING DEMOGRAPHIC INFORMATION

Gather census data for your community for your planning group to review. The U.S. Census Bureau conducts thorough studies of the demographics of each county and municipality. This data is usually available at a local public library or the chamber of commerce.

1. From the demographic information you have gathered, as well as any information you may have from other sources, what can you learn about the people in your community who are ages twenty to thirty-five? For example:

- What percentage is male and what is female?
- What is the racial/ethnic breakdown?
- Where do they live?
- How many are married and how many are single?
- How many are families with children?
- What education level have most attained?
- What is their employment status?
- What is the average income level?

2. How will this learning affect your ministry strategy?

LEARNING ABOUT POSTMODERN CULTURE AND GENERATION X

See Resources and Networks on pages 161–173. Decide on books you will read and people or organizations you will contact to learn more about postmodern culture and Generation X.

1. What are the most important things your team learned from the books you read and people you contacted?

2. How will this influence your ministry strategy?

DRAFTING A STRATEGIC MINISTRY PLAN

1. Write a brief description of your vision for your congregation's ministry with the postmodern community.

2. What three things do you wish for every person who comes in contact with your ministry?

3. What will you do to make those things possible?

4. Describe your vision for this ministry in these areas:

Evangelism   Worship
Hospitality   Discipleship

5. How will this ministry fit within your congregation's overall ministry strategy?

6. What present resources do you have available for this ministry?

Finances   Building space
Staff   Music and sound equipment
Volunteers
People for music and worship leadership

7. Where resources are lacking, what steps will you take to acquire them?

8. Briefly outline your strategy and a time line for implementing your ministry to Generation X.

9. How will you measure the effectiveness of your ministry?

chapter 3

Sharing *good news*

Pam Fickenscher

Pam serves as pastor of Spirit Garage, a congregation in Minneapolis, Minnesota, with more than one hundred participants and with an average age of twenty-eight.

Sonja was not someone who was afraid of much. A few years after college, she moved across the country on her own, sought out a new job in a different field, and began working her way through graduate school. She developed a new circle of friends, got involved in volunteer activities, and frequently spent her free time learning new skills or heading out on outdoor adventures. It was on such a trip that she was learning to rock climb with friends and a few professional instructors. She was having a wonderful time and as the day wore on, her confidence increased and her taste for the thrills of the heights were sharpened. Then, the unthinkable happened. Her harness snapped in midair, sending her plunging to the rock thirty feet below.

Miraculously, she landed in such a way that she could stand up again—at least for a moment. But the fall severely injured her back and knees, so that well into the next year she lived with chronic pain. But even more difficult for daily living was the emotional trauma. Post-traumatic stress disorder left her dealing with frequent attacks of panic or depression. She questioned why this had happened, and why she was even alive at all. Her joy in life and new things faded as she pondered the fact that she might easily have died that day. Moreover, Sonja struggled with the possible legal ramifications of the fall. Her instructors had clearly been negligent, failing to check her harness adequately. Some of her friends encouraged her to sue for pain and suffering as well as medical expenses, but she remained uncertain whether such action would alleviate her stress or merely exacerbate it.

Throughout this time Sonja carried on conversations with God, although she had never been part of any organized religion. She was unfamiliar with Christian beliefs; a few friends occasionally shared their views in bits and pieces, but their particular system of Christian belief didn't fit into her worldview. She even attended worship services a few times with a friend, but was uncomfortable with the worship style and unsettled by the theology. Nevertheless, she prayed frequently about the aftermath of the accident, asking for guidance in dealing with both the physical pain and the practical legal decisions.

Finally, longing for some kind of resolution, Sonja set up a meeting with the climbing instructors, though she was not at all sure what she would say. Before the meeting, she prayed for guidance. She didn't have a "religious" vocabulary, so she simply prayed, "Help me out with this. I don't know what I'm going to say."

The meeting was tense, and it was clear that the instructors expected her to sue. They discussed the accident and its aftermath, her medical expenses, and the physical therapy that still lay ahead of her. She was assertive, insisting that they were responsible for the accident and should at least cover her medical costs. But what followed surprised even Sonja. "I'm not going to sue you," she said. Their jaws dropped as it became clear that she wasn't going to pursue any claims for emotional damages.

To this day Sonja tells the story with surprise in her voice. "I went in to that meeting because I felt like I was going mad. I asked God to show me what to do and what to say because I couldn't make sense of why on earth I had instigated the meeting or why I felt like that was the thing to do. I just wanted some sort of assistance with all the medical bills that had piled up. I was as surprised as everyone else with what came out of my mouth. And then, when I got up to leave, I turned to the instructor who should have been the one to catch the mistake, and I said, "Can I give you a hug?"

Looking back on that moment, Sonja says "There was an incredible sense of peace and my heart really grew. I knew that everything would be OK—not to say that it would be easy—from that moment on. And I have to believe that that moment also healed my instructor. All I know is, I did the right thing for me. I don't want to even think about the kind of person I may have become had I gone the route that was expected."

Shortly after this time, Sonja heard about a new church in her community that focused on outreach to postmodern generations. Called Spirit Garage, the community described itself as "the church with the really big door." At the time Sonja heard of the community, they met on Sunday mornings in a small comedy theater for worship. The music was rock and blues-based; no one dressed up for the gatherings, and the community was engaged in hands-on service projects in the neighborhood.

Sonja joined in the life of Spirit Garage as she did everything else before the accident—jumping in with both feet. She quickly got involved in service projects, then started attending small-group meetings—first one geared toward the basics of Christianity, then a women's small group, then a group for preparation for baptism. She still has many questions about the intellectual basis of Christianity and the purpose of organized religion, but she has found a home there. Without hesitation she will say that God led her to Spirit Garage. Now she is organizing others at the church to learn rock climbing, and soon she plans to be baptized—outdoors, where she says she continues to feel God's presence the most powerfully.

WHAT IS GOD UP TO?

One of the working assumptions of ministry to people like Sonja—postmoderns, or Generation X, is that God is at work in many ways in people's lives, long before they ever may enter a church community. When they encounter people with Christian commitments, Generation Xers will ask whether the language being used to describe God and spirituality matches with their own experiences of life. Like seekers of every time, Xers are often most open to God's spirit and an alternate view of the world when their own coping mechanisms have been stretched to the limit. This is no different than with previous generations, but the importance of recognizing God's movement outside the usual evangelistic methods and church-sponsored events is particularly important because Xers may lack any other means of interpreting their pasts. Ministries that seek to reach them must be prepared to help Xers deal with the fear and distrust from their past as well as offer a meaningful model of community for the present. The question those who minister to Generation Xers must constantly be asking, both privately and publicly, is: What is God doing in our midst?

The first and best way to discover some answers to such a big question is silence and listening. Before any pastor or community reaches out to Xers or the generations that follow them, we need to humbly admit that God's ways are not our ways, and that we may not immediately know what God is already doing in the lives of others.

Working assumptions for evangelism

There is a good bit of irony in talking about "assumptions" or "principles" of postmodern evangelism, because for many people thinking like a Gen Xer will mean they have to stop assuming that they know what this generation wants. Any "principles" of postmodern ministry are based more on opening up possibilities than on limiting the ways in which we go about ministry with and for this generation. Ideally this chapter would be presented as a Web site, with multiple connections, interlinked stories, and numerous entry points. But for now, we work in a linear format to fit the medium, hoping the reader will understand that there ought to be a link, or at least a footnote, qualifying and modifying every one of these principles.

Assumption 1. God has been working in people's lives long before they walk through the church door. Sonja had a compelling experience of God's guidance and the power of forgiveness before she entered a Christian community that could put language and a framework around that experience. When we talk about God to unchurched people in a postmodern context, we must assume that our structures for evangelism, whatever they are, will never fully encompass what God may be doing in the minds and hearts of people searching for faith. Just as Xers resist generational labels in the first place, they also resist being "typed" or categorized spiritually. In our community, the typical member of Spirit Garage might be described as one who is offended at the idea of being typical. Though carefully designed, complicated methods of making visitors into members and ministers will be resisted.

Assumption 2. There is no single entry point to faith. While any good evangelist wants to bring people into vital relationship with Jesus Christ, in our postmodern culture we cannot assume that faith will "happen" by any one means. Some people, like Sonja, will be attracted to the community and become very attached long before they are ready to make a public profession of faith through baptism. Some ministries respond to this by creating "low-threshold" worship experiences, ones that do not assume any visitor participation at all. Other ministries have weekly communion anyway, with the understanding that the table itself is inviting, even to those who do not fully understand its theological basis. Beyond worship, many postmodern ministries create invitational events that involve Xers in service projects, open discussion about faith designed for seekers, or other activities that do not require a previous understanding of or commitment to Christian faith. This "side door" approach may be the most difficult for faith traditions that emphasize making a decision for Christ, and for churches with a clear, linear model for incorporation into the faith community. Think carefully about how your congregation's understanding of conversion fits with a postmodern mindset. (See the "Tradition Analysis" worksheet.)

TRADITION ANALYSIS

I. What does my tradition say theologically about conversion?

- Is it a process or a single decision? Is it intellectual, emotional, or a choice or all of the above?

- Are there key words we look for that mark a testimony as genuine?

- Do those words make sense to people who are unchurched, or are they strictly "code" for insiders?

2. What does my congregation say implicitly about conversion?

- Do we have a process for seekers to engage in? Do we invite people explicitly to a decision?

- Do we regularly acknowledge that not everyone present is already a believer?

- Do we acknowledge that even long-time members have faith struggles and questions?

3. How does our membership process correspond to our theology of conversion? Do we assume that most new members will be transfers from other congregations of the same tradition or Christians from another tradition?

4. If the average person will take more than a year to make a commitment to the community, and perhaps at least that long to make a commitment to Christ, do our explicit and implicit messages about conversion allow space for that process?

Assumption 3. There is no single entry point to community. The people of Generation X are often more comfortable entering the church by the "side door" rather than the front. Service projects, social action, or retreat settings, rather than Sunday worship, may be a person's first contact with a church community. Some Xers will test a community for an extensive period before making a public profession of faith, and some will think of themselves as "members" without ever seeking to formalize that relationship. While many Xers will welcome opportunities to ritualize their connections to the community, an emphasis on signing a piece of paper—even a membership covenant focused on prayer, worship, and stewardship—may be viewed as too institutional. Adults who were baptized as children may appreciate an opportunity to reaffirm their baptismal promises but step around a "membership process" that appears too corporate.

Assumption 4. Generation Xers may enter into a vital, prayerful relationship with Jesus long before they are ready to commit to him. While many Christians define faith itself by its exclusive commitment to one God in Jesus Christ, Xers are likely to seek experiences of faith and spirituality for an extensive testing period, whereas their Baby Boomer counterparts will test intellectually, participating only when they are ready to say "I believe." Xers will participate readily while holding open the door to other worldviews and faiths at the same time. A ministry focused to Xers therefore will need to sensitively discuss the relationship of Christianity to other faiths, worldviews, and commitments, and be ready to admit where it has confused its own internal culture or U.S. Protestant worldview with the essentials of the faith.

Assumption 5. We can never know all that is going on in the human heart. Certainly this is a good assumption for any ministry, but it is especially pertinent to generation-focused ministries. No amount of research into a generational cohort or culture can provide us with exhaustive insight into a particular person's faith development. This remains a highly individual process.

BELIEF IS NOT THE PROBLEM

Many twentieth-century evangelism efforts were based on the assumption that non-Christians needed to overcome a resistance to belief itself. The task of the church was to make Christian belief sensible, approachable, reasonable, even "scientific." Churches would distribute pamphlets and Bibles with the hope that the Holy Spirit would work on an individual mind and heart to produce faith in the absence of community. Faith formation for young people in mainline churches usually involved memorizing rational explanations of Scripture, the creeds, and the Ten Commandments. Once they could "put it into their own words," the process of faith formation was considered complete. And frequently these efforts were effective for people who approached the world in a modern, rational way. During the 1970s and '80s many seeker-oriented churches modeled their preaching and education after seminars in the business world, providing fill-in-the-blank outlines and point-by-point illustrations of the basics of Christian belief. Many Baby Boomer churches continue in this model with some effectiveness with those whose minds and social worlds were formed in the era of Sputnik.

For Generation Xers, however, the obstacle to faith is not science, misinformation, or "unbelief" in the modern sense of that word. We may very well convince a Gen Xer that Jesus lived, died, and rose again. They will then shrug and say, "So?" Xers are eager to believe in something that will give their lives meaning, particularly if that belief can be experienced in either a mystical or pragmatic way.

While Gen Xers understand that you can't believe everything you read, their basic mistrust in anyone's truth does not mean that they avoid believing at all. Consider the following e-mail, passed around the Internet in 1999:

> "I know this guy whose neighbor, a young man, was home recovering from having been served a rat in his bucket of

Kentucky Fried Chicken. So anyway, one day he went to sleep and when he awoke he was in his bathtub and it was full of ice and he was sore all over. When he got out of the tub he realized that HIS KIDNEYS HAD BEEN STOLEN and he saw a note on his mirror that said "Call 911!" But he was afraid to use his phone because it was connected to his computer, and there was a virus on his computer that would destroy his hard drive if he opened an e-mail entitled "Join the crew!" He knew it wasn't a hoax because he himself was a computer programmer who was working on software to save us from Armageddon when the year 2000 rolls around. His program would prevent a global disaster in which all the computers get together and distribute the $600 Neiman Marcus cookie recipe under the leadership of Bill Gates. (It's true—I read it all last week in a mass e-mail from BILL GATES HIMSELF, who was also promising me a free Disney World vacation and $5,000 if I would forward the e-mail to everyone I knew.)

The message continues for another full page, combining urban myth, e-mail hoaxes, and dark bizarre stories.

Gen Xers are just as likely as anyone else to believe these myths, hoaxes, and dire predictions about the future—although perhaps they have become a bit more suspicious before passing on the latest tale. What is more common is a basic mistrust in human institutions, so that the church may be the very last place they will go to find belief. A congregation that has a clear sign out front, regular notices in the "church section" of the local newspaper and an ad in the Yellow Pages may wonder why it doesn't get more visitors. The reason is simple—most Generation Xers are not "looking for" a church. They may be trying on belief systems, alternative therapies, new identities, and relationships at a frenetic pace, but the institution of the church is the last place they would seek out to find community, identity, or, ultimately, faith.

The first step in evangelism with Gen Xers, therefore, will not be convincing anyone of your argument. As Christian individuals and communities, we need to realize that for many Gen Xers we are the message. The first step is to build relationships in such a way that conversations over the deeper meaning of life and the possibility of faith and commitment will develop. Gen Xers, in other words, need to have relationships of integrity modeled for them, so that faith in a reliable, loving God might become an intelligible possibility.

IDENTITY AND INTEGRITY

The difficulty for many mainline Christians, unaccustomed as we are to sharing our faith, is to imagine ourselves as evangelists without thinking we have to take on either the crass language of marketers on the one hand, or the fire-and-brimstone language of fundamentalists on the other. You may be relieved to realize that if you become clear about who you are in relationship to God and to people who are unchurched, you will not have to take on an "alternative identity" in order to become an effective evangelist. What is required is not a whole new theology, language, technology, or even a tattoo, but simply a bit of self-examination.

Who am I? A sinner

About one year into the task of building a new postmodern congregation, I had a dream that we had been wildly successful. Our auditorium, which seats six hundred, was nearly full, and people were attentive and expectant as I preached and moved into the communion liturgy. Then I looked down at the communion table and found that there was neither bread nor wine for the feast. This being a dream, I sent one of our volunteers to the grocery store, and the entire crowd patiently waited for him to return. After fifteen, thirty, then forty-five minutes he finally came back, and we reconvened for the feast. As I leaned forward slightly toward the table, my hair caught in the flames of our candles. The entire congregation watched and was oddly silent as my head caught on fire.

Regardless of how well-prepared we are, the process of reaching out to postmodern generations will cause us to come face-to-face with our own limitations, mixed motives, and sinfulness. We will inevitably encounter moments when the task will seem overwhelming and the resources available to it meager. The practice of daily confession and self-examination is a vital piece of faith formation, not so much because God needs to hear our sins but because as Christians we need the daily reminder of why God's grace is necessary at all. As individuals and as a community our preparation to reach out must include self-examination and confession, lest we not encounter our own mixed motives until they do some damage.

This acknowledgment that we are sinners does not stop once we are engaged in building a new community. It must continue to be a practice where pastors and lay people, baptized and seeker alike, are willing to stand before God as sinners. Rather than be scared off by talk of sin, many Xers are relieved to find a community where pain, failings, and guilt are openly acknowledged in an atmosphere of trust and compassion.

Postmodern theology requires not only that we acknowledge our status as sinners, but also that we acknowledge our limitations as interpreters of the Word and friends of God. Evangelism in the postmodern world and beyond will demand that we face up to contradictions and questions that in the modern era were smoothed away in the name of consistency and mastery. In the article "The Dance of Truth" in the *Mars Hill Review*, Don Hudson tells about a theology professor, teaching his class about postmodern biblical interpretation, who wrote on the blackboard "Rule #1." As the class waited to write down the rule, he turned around and said simply, "I am wrong." Postmodern biblical study, as well as evangelism, must be prepared to say not only "I have sinned," but also, "I am wrong" (*Mars Hill Review*, No. 12, Fall 1998, p. 19).

Who am I? A saint

In the movie *Leaving Normal*, a curious contest takes place between the two main characters. One woman has floated around the country from place to place most of her life, failing to find a faithful relationship, meaningful work, or a place to call home; another woman has just left a dead-end job as a bartender in a small town and is relishing her new freedom. The two become traveling companions and, in classic road movie style, become fast friends as they head west. One evening their conversations begin to reveal more of their pasts. The younger woman, played by Meg Tilly, insists that she is a horrible person, and goes on to list her mistakes and foibles. Her older travel companion, played by Christine Lahti, matches every failing with one of her own. The debate escalates until Lahti lays out her trump card, "I abandoned my own child as a baby." The younger woman gasps and falls silent as her friend bitterly says, "Bingo, I win."

The irony of Christian confession in an age of public displays of personal failing and voyeuristic talk shows is that most of the culture responds to our admission of fault with a simple, "So?" Because the culture believes in confession without absolution— free speech without accountability, Christians may be tempted to go beyond mere honesty about their spiritual journeys to a sort of false humility that denies God's transformative power in our lives. Small groups can easily slip into patterns of competing horror stories unless the practice of gratitude is also thoroughly ingrained into church life. Put in theological terms, outreach that does not claim our status as sanctified (transformed) as well as justified (saved) will miss the mark in a postmodern world. Anyone can talk about their struggles with the big questions of life; and most of us, if we are honest, will admit that we don't have all the answers, but only those who follow Christ can say they have found the Way.

While the church certainly has a great deal in its history to be humble about, many Christians become downright apologetic about their personal faith as well. The practice of testimony has died out in many white mainline congregations, to the point that even within congregations we have the impression that personal faith is a private matter. The consequences for the church are that we not only fail to witness to people who are unchurched, we also lose our sense of gratitude and mutual celebration for what God is doing in our midst among the faithful. While your ministry with Generation X will demand a humility and willingness to be open and vulnerable, it also demands an equal measure of open gratitude and joy that God has brought you through the trials of the past. Both worship and personal witness can then take on the pattern of law and gospel, confession and praise.

Who am I? A friend

Charlene Cox, campus minister for a large state university, tells the story of a young man who was known for his piercings—ears, nose, eyebrow, tongue. This man's piercings not only set him apart "decoratively," they expressed something about his approach to life—an unflinching tolerance of pain. He got to know the community of students in the campus ministry, and one day announced that he was going in for yet another piercing. And then, a bit of challenge in his voice, he demanded, "Who's going with me?" For this young man, whose piercings were just the external expression of lots of life pain, the invitation to piercing was a challenge to friendship. Regardless of what else they thought of him, he needed to know whether these friends would walk with him through this expression of his pain.

An outreach to Xers, like an outreach to any other generation, must respond to the perceived needs of the seeker. The difference between a Boomer outreach and a postmodern one, however, is that Xers generally do not think they need or want answers to life's problems. Such a claim will probably be viewed with suspicion by an Xer. At best, they think you are simple-minded; at worst, you're selling a bill of goods.

Most Xers have grown up in an atmosphere where cultural pluralism is a daily reality. They have formed friendships across cultural and ethnic lines and believe that only the values of friendship can transcend the differences between individuals. In order to demonstrate the truth of the gospel to a Gen Xer, you need not have all the answers, but you must be prepared to be a companion, a friend.

Friendship for the Gen Xer is an expression of loyalty and steadfastness that goes beyond mere agreement about values or beliefs. Gen Xers seek companions who will not abandon them when jobs, family relationships, or dating situations inevitably change. Because such steadfastness is unusually difficult to find, Gen Xers will be drawn to communities that offer unconditional love in demonstrable, pragmatic ways. These need not be professional services; in fact, the relational bias of this generation demands that any service offered, no matter how skilled, be offered as friend to friend, rather than professional to client or provider to customer. (See the "What Can We Do to Help?" worksheet.)

In witnessing to people of this generation, Christians need not shy away from the reality that the way of Jesus includes suffering as well as glory. Emotional pain is a familiar companion, so much so that many people of younger generations express their inward troubles in outward, sometimes grotesque, ways. Tattoos and piercings are the most socially acceptable forms of such expression, but eating disorders and "cutting" (compulsive drawing of blood by scraping or cutting with knives or razor blades) are alarmingly common signs of deep emotional pain. Christians need to witness that because of Christ we expect to walk with our brothers and sisters through pain; and yet we believe that by the power of the resurrection, pain will not have the final word.

Amid this concern for relational ministry and personal vulnerability, we must not forget that ministry for Gen Xers, like any Christian ministry, must respect personal boundaries and hold high ethical standards. Ministry in the postmodern era may easily blur the lines between preacher and listener, between teacher and student. These blurred boundaries can open new doors to ministry and strengthen both church communities and individuals. Unfortunately, the church also often assumes the one strict barrier,

WHAT CAN WE DO TO HELP?

Looking at our community, what are the ways our congregation can offer friendship?

1. What are the situations where young adults are open to and needing friendship and help?

Realities of young adult life:
• Job hunting/Career discernment
• Addiction/Substance abuse
• Self-care/Health
• Moving/Apartment hunting/ Relocation
• Dating/Relationship building
• Financial struggles/Debt management
• Education/Finishing degrees
• First-time home ownership (in some cases)
• Marriage and parenting (for some)

2. What resources does our congregation have to offer people with these issues?
• People with expertise (accountants, counselors)
• People with life experience (marriage, parenting)
• People with similar struggles
• People with time/muscle power (for example, to help with moving)
• People with access to information (Where are the affordable apartments? What companies are hiring?)

3. What are our means to make these services available?

• Free seminars	• Web site networking
• Community bulletin boards	• Classified ads
• Support groups	• Walk-in counseling
• Other:	

which is still maintained in American culture—the wall between private and public. The church has suffered many public wounds due to leaders who have thought they were immune from temptation and ended up in inappropriate relationships with parishioners. The church must continue to be vigilant about modeling healthy, appropriate personal boundaries. This applies not only to thinking carefully about intimate relationships, but also to the ways in which leaders share their own struggles. Preachers who share personal pain should consistently ask themselves, "Why am I sharing this?" One rule of thumb is to ask, "Is this an issue that I feel I have come to some resolution about, or am I making myself vulnerable here for my benefit, hoping for sympathy and support?" Making oneself vulnerable should feel risky because it is humbling to be known as a wounded healer, not because it crosses lines that may lead to unhealthy interactions. These skills of discerning healthy boundaries must also be consciously taught to lay leaders, lest evangelists with ulterior motives give Xers yet another reason to distrust the church.

Who am I? A servant

"Free?" the caller asked. "Do I have to join the church?"

"No ma'am, it's just a meal we want to offer to the community."

"So should I bring something? Like a potluck?"

"No, ma'am the food is all provided."

"So, do I have to volunteer or something to get the meal?"

"No, no. It's just our gift to the community. It's free."

"But why are you doing this?"

"We just want to give something back as God has given to us. Free of charge. We want to celebrate Easter with the community."

The idea of grace, of a truly free gift, is foreign to our society. No matter what their age, most Americans are suspicious of someone who offers something for nothing. We do not believe there is a free lunch, and therefore find it hard to believe in a God who would be so generous as to offer forgiveness and grace for nothing.

Unfortunately, many of our efforts at evangelism do not reflect this radical belief in God's grace. In his book *Conspiracy of Kindness*, Steve Sjogren describes servant ministries at the congregation he serves in Cincinnati, Ohio, and argues that traditional efforts at evangelism and invitation are "high risk" and "low grace." They are high risk for most lay people in that they are uncomfortable with the idea of witnessing to strangers or "selling" something they are growing in themselves. At the same time, door-knocking leaflet ministries and other traditional means are "low grace" for the community because they present the faith in propositional, sometimes intrusive ways without providing an actual experience of what God's love is like (*Conspiracy of Kindness*, Steve Sjogren. Ann Arbor, Mich.: Vine Books, 1993.).

What might a "low risk, high grace" effort look like? Following the example of the Vineyard Fellowship of Cincinnati where Sjogren serves, many congregations take on servant ministries as a means to make contact with unchurched people. This may include everything from labor-intensive housing projects to simply passing out free sodas on a hot day. Lay people are instructed simply to give away a gift or a service and refuse any offers of payment. They engage people in conversation if—and only if—the recipients themselves want to know, "Why are you doing this?" Then, when the message we want to share has actually been asked for, we are prepared to say, "because of what Christ has done for us."

Servant ministries can take on many forms. Many congregations already involved in social ministries have built-in opportunities to offer "low-risk, high grace" messages. What prevents us is that often we think of these ministries as separate from evangelism, as service that will not bear the fruit of faith in those who witness it. By simply reintegrating these efforts as means to both show and tell about your faith, you may find that your community grows both larger in number and deeper in commitment to the Great Commission.

These "high grace, low risk" ministries need not be program-oriented. That is, one need not develop an organized small group or major event around servant ministry. Rather, this attitude can be worked into teaching, preaching, and existing congregational ministry. They may also develop by teaching individuals in the community to pray for their unchurched friends and to witness in friendship and one-on-one servanthood. One large congregation in South Korea encouraged each of its members to pick a coworker or a friend to pray for and serve over the course of many weeks. The idea simply was to pay attention to this individual, to make a point of offering compliments, doing favors, being present in times of need. No further witnessing was required unless the individual asked, "Why?" Within only four months, most of those identified persons had become Christians.

While servanthood can take on either very public or very personal modes, either way it must be clear that these efforts are not merely instrumental. We do not become advocates for the poor in order to "win" for our cause; nor do we act as servants toward our neighbors only to "win" their souls or their good favor toward our church. We behave as servants toward one another and toward the world because that is what Jesus commanded us to do. We believe in so doing, we will become more like him. Jesus made it clear that those who serve the least of these will often not recognize him as they are doing so (Matthew 25), but in serving they will be meeting him. And just as we expect to meet him on the streets, we should not be surprised when he then shows up at our community table, hungry and longing for fellowship.

HOSPITALITY

Hospitality is not the committee that provides coffee on Sunday morning; it is the base principle of every outreach effort, be it social ministry, advertising, a new worship service, or a new mission start. Jesus' most common radical practice was eating with sinners, showing compassion and friendship before he urged them to change. Whether it is a cup of coffee with a prospective member, serving a meal at a homeless shelter, or welcoming people to the Lord's Supper in worship, a ministry to Xers must constantly keep its eye on this "come as you are" starting point of all relationships.

The fact that Gen Xers seek faithful friendships, intensity, and "realness" does not necessarily mean that the most outgoing, hyper-friendly congregations will be the most successful in drawing them in. On the contrary, Gen Xers value their privacy as much as the next person, and many prefer to by anonymous when they first enter a new community. Rick Warren, pastor of a large church in Orange County, California, has noted that most Americans list "talking in front of people" and "being at a party surrounded by strangers" as among their top fears. And yet many churches, in an effort to be friendly, put newcomers on the spot by insisting that guests introduce themselves publicly (*The Purpose Driven Church*, Richard Warren. Grand Rapids, Mich.: Zondervan Publishing, 1995)! True hospitality does not insist that every visitor become immediately known or involved, but lets the guest set the pace.

Some communities are explicit about the kind of hospitality they offer. Some issue the invitation to a new worship service expressly to singles or twenty-somethings, sometimes even asking that parents or older members attend another church. Other congregations phrase their invitation more in terms of attitude than age or marital status. Language, music, and atmosphere set the tone, allowing visitors to select whether this is the place for them. Spirit Garage sets this tone with its "rules," read at the beginning of worship on a regular basis.

Spirit Garage rules

I. Be honest. Don't stand up, sit up, speak up, dress up, cheer up, or buck up unless the Spirit moves you. God knows if you're lying, and you won't have as much fun.

2. Pay attention. If this is the only hour a week you give your soul, make it count.

3. When all else fails (and preferably long before that), pray.

4. We know this isn't a garage. It's a metaphor, a metaphor, okay?

5. Please, no pantyhose.

Through a visitor's eyes

In preparing a community or individuals to act hospitably, it is particularly helpful to have regular attendees attempt to understand what a first-time visitor's experience is like. One exercise is to attend other congregations—especially those of different traditions or denominations—and take notes on the experience. (See "Experiencing Church as a Visitor.") Another is to attempt an incognito experience at your own congregation, again taking notes to share with others later. This usually works the best when you can ask a friend who genuinely doesn't know his or her way around and who truly won't be recognized. Finally, you can ask visitors themselves for some feedback. Many churches do this with visitor cards or follow-up letters, allowing visitors a simple and quick way to respond to their experiences. These work best if postage is provided and the visitor can answer anonymously. (See "How Was It?" sample visitor card.)

After you have considered how any first-time visitor might respond, solicit feedback in whatever way you can from younger people themselves, preferably those who have not been raised in the congregation. People of postmodern generations tend to have a different visceral response to hospitality than Baby Boomers. Anything that appears too organized, too orchestrated, or "slick" will not be trusted. The coffee may be great, the smiles big and the building immaculate, but an Xer may still conclude, "I don't belong here." Congregations may have to try out several "moods" and "attitudes" before they find one that fits the life situation of Xers in their community. Finding the best way to communicate this authentic interest will depend on the congregation's size, context, and tradition, but should always be done with an ear to the experience of actual visitors.

EXPERIENCING CHURCH AS A VISITOR

Complete this questionnaire after you have visited another congregation. Or ask someone to visit your congregation and then answer these questions.

Facilities

1. Was the worship facility easy to find? Did the map and/or verbal directions to the church correspond to your knowledge of the neighborhood?

2. How was parking? Could you find a parking place easily? Were there signs or people to direct you?

3. Was the front door easy to find? If the entrance to the worship space was not immediately evident, was the signage clear?

4. Were signs or directions to the restrooms posted?

5. Was there an information table or a clear way to find out more about the congregation?

People

1. Did anyone greet you when you arrived? Did he or she offer a name or wear a name tag?

2. Were you offered a bulletin or order of service or other assistance to help you follow and participate in worship?

3. Were others able to direct you when you had questions about the facility or the service?

Food

1. If any food or drink was offered, was it clearly visible?

2. Did anyone who greeted you personally offer coffee, or another beverage, or snacks?

Children

1. Did you feel that your children were as welcomed as you were?

2. Were there clear messages about whether children are welcome in worship or whether childcare is available?

3. If there was childcare available, was the facility adequate?

4. Would you feel safe leaving your child in the room and with the childcare workers while you worshiped?

5. If children were welcomed and encouraged to be present during the worship service, how did other worshipers react to their presence?

Worship service

1. Did you feel you could navigate your way through the worship service?

2. Were any instructions or welcomes given specifically to first-time visitors?

3. Were announcements given in the worship that were understandable to newcomers?

4. If the Lord's Supper was offered at worship, was the congregation's policy about who is welcome to commune made clear?

Beyond thinking about the generic person's response to hospitality, congregations should think about visiting through the eyes of people in specific life situations. For example, how would someone who is single and lonely feel in your service? How would a person who is struggling to pay his rent respond? Would someone who is sight-impaired feel welcomed and relatively comfortable? If a homosexual couple came to visit, would they be welcomed or stared at? Would someone who has experienced abuse feel safe? Would someone new in town know how to make sense of the community announcements?

Many Generation X ministries have found that the metaphor of a living room is a helpful image for the atmosphere they try to create. The Gathering, a church within a church at Ginghamsburg United Methodist Church in Tipp City, Ohio, has an old sofa as its icon. The idea of a living room reminds members that they are the hosts while communicating a "come as you are" message to visitors. Food and drink are offered as an essential piece of welcoming the stranger. The music is not unlike what you might listen to at home, and the worship, while planned, still has a relaxed, conversational feel to it. Churches that create a living room atmosphere often find that their visitors are more tolerant of mistakes and imperfections because they do not feel they are attending a production. If a Gen Xer tells you your church feels real, she has paid you the highest compliment.

EXTERNAL COMMUNICATIONS

Many established churches, unaccustomed to being overlooked in their communities, recoil at the idea of advertising their presence. Advertising, however, is simply one form of "hanging out your shingle." Unless people know you exist, they cannot visit. External communications are the signage of any community, but that signage takes on many forms and locations for the postmodern church. Twenty-first century America is so overloaded with information, the church has to do much more than hang out a shingle. Focused ministries that truly have evangelism as their goal must think creatively and contextually about where people in their area who are unchurched sleep, eat, work, and socialize. You must think about what kinds of invitations will be most readily noticed and accepted, and then selectively aim your efforts at advertising and invitation. Certainly, some experimentation will be necessary, but the best starting point is just to ask. Striving to be the learner in matters of publicity and marketing will at least earn you some unlikely allies and at most provide professional assistance in competing with all the other messages out there.

HOW WAS IT?
Sample visitor card

Send this card to first-time visitors with return postage.
There is no need to identify the visitor.

Were you greeted by anyone when you arrived?

My favorite piece of music was . . .

The message was . . .

How did you hear about us?

Do you currently attend any church?

Any suggestions?

Prayer requests:

Do your research

In addition to the listening exercises from chapters in this book, a
team might look very specifically at the messages they hear and see
communicated about church, Christians, and organized religion in
the local culture as well as in the mass media. Typical messages
include:

Message 1. "Church is for losers." With the exception of Mother
Teresa, religion is seldom associated with the most admired or
successful figures of our culture.

Message 2. "Organized religion is not for me"—or its corollary:
"Church is not spiritual enough." The dichotomy of spirituality vs.
religion in popular thought puts the responsibility on churches to
redefine their purposes in a way that communicates their spiritual
significance for seekers.

Message 3. "I don't trust organizations." Actually, this is not true. Most Xers do trust organizations, such as companies or other employers—at least to pay them next week—but not to care about their well-being or their future. Many postmodern churches therefore draw on biblical language to describe their community life and steer away from traditional organizational terms. One postmodern congregation refers to this on their Web site simply as "body life," emphasizing the biblical understanding of life together.

Message 4. "Churches are only concerned about themselves." Gen Xers will be attracted to a congregation that communicates a vision much bigger than its own promotion or survival. Many Gen Xers believe in individualism for themselves, but that doesn't mean that they will openly approve of it in anyone else.

Message 5. "Christians are all judgmental." Regardless of whether they know about Jesus' teachings to remove the log from a person's own eye first, the majority of unchurched Xers assume all Christians have a "holier than thou" attitude.

Message 6. "I don't know what I believe. Church people seem to have made up their minds." Sadly, many Gen Xers think that the church is the last place they would go to carry on a spiritual search. One person who invited a friend to our congregation was told, "I'm not a congregation kind of person." "That's OK," she responded, "We're not really congregation kind of people either!" Xers might even be interested in Christianity and drawn by the stories of Jesus, but they don't believe (sometimes rightly) that their questions will be welcomed within a church community.

Note your competition

Pay attention to agencies, companies, books, and resources that purport to offer health, wholeness, well-being, or personal growth. When popular spirituality has outstripped traditional religion in the public eye, the church has some serious questions to ask. Are we communicating Jesus' healing and salvation in a language that

makes sense to our community, or are we too caught up in traditional theological categories from another era? Are we attentive to
the uniqueness of the church's mission, offering community as
well as personal growth, mission as well as needs-based ministries,
story as well as system?

Try new and varied means

Consider different means of communication. What are the venues
that are most often seen by your target crowd? Are you comfortable advertising in nontraditional places? For example, most
churches think of advertising in the Yellow Pages under
"churches," or perhaps on the designated church page of their local
newspaper. But who would be looking at these pages? Those who
are looking for a church, not those who are truly unchurched. If
you're not looking to buy a car, you won't go to the automotive
section of the newspaper. Brainstorm a bit about where someone
who isn't looking for church, but might need Christ, would see an
ad or article. (See "Evaluating Media Venues.")

Newspapers. Consider places outside the church section, such as
the classifieds: What if a church posted a personal ad? Or, contact
a reporter and send press releases about events you have planned.

Special interest publications. Many metropolitan areas have
weekly papers devoted to the interests of a particular ethnic group,
women's issues, or the arts.

"Alternative" papers. Many urban areas have an alternative weekly,
usually free, that lists club offerings, restaurants, the arts, and other
events of special interest to younger people. These are particularly
popular in larger urban areas with an active music and arts scene.
Because of their alternative flavor, their readership tends to be
high, not only among Gen Xers but also among people of other
generations who think in postmodern terms.

University/Community college newspapers. Most schools seek
outside advertising to pay for their publishing costs.

Neighborhood newspapers/newsletters. Many neighborhood papers offer reasonable advertising rates, and their reporters are often hungry for off-beat news about community goings-on. Writers for these publications can be helpful contacts simply for keeping a finger on the pulse of a neighborhood, although their interests are sometimes biased toward homeowners and business owners.

Billboards. Some churches have had great success with off-beat "signs from God."

Flyers. while some urban areas have laws against posting flyers on telephone poles, many coffee houses, running paths, health clubs, community colleges, grocery stores, and other public places have community bulletin boards. This is a labor-intensive, but low-cost and grassroots way of getting the word out.

Radio. Note that radio is one of the most age-, ethnicity-, and gender-segregated forms of mass media. Ask for demographic information and choose your venue carefully. The hard rock station, for example, is likely to have a mostly white male (and often over twenty-five) audience. Also think strategically about timing. If you live in a downtown community where most students and workers take the bus, bike, or walk to a downtown job, drive-time ads will not reach your target audience.

Cable television. Is there a public access station in your area?

Direct mail. This is an extremely popular mode of advertising for new Baby Boomer churches, particularly because new homeowners are an easy market to track, and they have relatively stable social habits. The jury is still out whether this is an equally effective technique with Generation Xers.

Telemarketing. It's been done, but losing effectiveness in the '90s. Few people recommend it in the age of caller ID and mass marketing weariness.

EVALUATING MEDIA VENUES

1. Which media reach our target audience?

2. What are the financial costs involved?

3. Can your congregation afford to use this medium more than once? How easy and/or effective would it be to repeat the same message in this medium over time, such as monthly ads in the same publication or quarterly mailings to the same neighborhood?

4. What are the risks of a negative response? Would a negative response cut a person off from our ministry? (In other words, a phone call saying "Take me off your list!") Would a negative response demoralize your current members?

5. What is the "life" of the medium? (Remember, even daily print media can easily be saved, whereas television or radio ads are less likely to have a lasting reminder.)

6. How much control do we have over the message? (Solicited articles may misrepresent your purpose, while direct mail gives you complete control.)

7. Is the medium active or passive? For example, radio ads are passive—they do not require the person to read, respond, or open anything; a telemarketing call is active—it forces a response from the person on the other end.

Print media

Local newspaper

Church section

Other places for advertising

Articles

Special interest periodicals

Special interest local directories

"Alternative" papers

College/university newspapers

Neighborhood newspapers/newsletters

"Newcomer"/real estate guides/apartment listings

Yellow Pages (Don't forget Internet yellow pages)

Public venues

Billboards

Flyers

Open mikes at concerts/ poetry slams

Servant events

Web site

Other mass media

Radio

Cable TV

TV news

Direct campaigns

Direct mail

Telemarketing

Door knocking

"Welcome Wagon" efforts

8. How much initiative does the public have to take to see or hear this message?

9. What elements of our ministry are best represented in this medium? (For example, a music publication might emphasize your alternative worship style.)

Word of mouth. Your most powerful communication tool. (See the section on internal communications, page 91.)

Guerrilla marketing. This term was coined by the marketing industry to describe advertisements deliberately placed in "out of place" venues. Examples for a church might include a personal ad in the romance section of the classifieds, coasters left at a bar with the church's information on it, or business cards posted on a professional board for massage therapists.

Learn from your attempts

Try something, and watch the response carefully. If you don't already have a system for finding out how the word is spreading about your congregation, get one. (See "How Was It?" sample visitor card.) Regularly evaluate how effective your various means of advertising really are, paying attention not only to gross numbers of visitors, but also whether visitors are coming back. In other words, which venues are drawing the attention of visitors who are likely to stay?

Ask the target audience

On a regular basis, test your communications with people who are unchurched. Find people who are not familiar with your ministry and ask them to evaluate how helpful and attractive your communications really are.

INTERNAL COMMUNICATIONS

Within the congregation, there are other levels of communication. Many churches approach Sunday morning as an insiders meeting, forgetting that even new members may still see themselves as outsiders. Public messages in sermons, teaching, newsletters, and the like need to continually keep this kind of mixed audience in mind. Never assume too much knowledge about the church's mission, the Bible, or what "Christian" itself means.

Among congregational leaders, there can be more freedom in talking about specific audiences, transforming worldview and "marketing" strategy. Many lay people are comfortable with such language from their business experience, but may need help in translating what is to some people crass terminology of market to a mission-driven, people-oriented understanding of ministry. While identifying a "target" is a helpful process for any marketing campaign, the success of that campaign in a church will not be whether it "hits its target" so much as whether it opens new doors to relationship.

Congregational goals and events

As noted before, the fact that Generation Xers process information differently from their predecessors poses a challenge for ministries that are accustomed to relying on traditional print media. This is especially true when communicating informatively. Many Gen Xers simply won't read a print newsletter even if it appears in their mailbox monthly. Thick sheets of "congregation events" will go unexamined unless there is a verbal invitation to attend. But no one wants to sit through twenty minutes of announcements every Sunday, so you must be creative about how to get out the word about significant congregation events. Some ministries use phone trees for important announcements. Many churches are now using e-mail newsletters to deliver news—often directly to Xers at their workplaces, where it's less likely to be lost in a pile of mail. Web-based newsletters have the advantage of being low-cost, nonlinear, colorful and easy to update, but may not reach your whole audience. Moreover, unlike e-mail, they require the reader to take the initiative in seeking out the site. One way around this is to send the site itself in the e-mail message. (See "How Do They Know? Analyzing Internal Communications.")

Because Gen Xers, like most people in the United States and Canada, are flooded with information daily, churches of the future will need to constantly reevaluate how they communicate internally with their members.

Existing networks

The easiest way to build a generationally-focused ministry is to tap into networks that already exist. The most obvious example is campus ministries, or ministries located near a college campus. University Baptist Church of Waco, Texas, though not an officially sanctioned campus group, got its start by spreading the word among the students and recent graduates of nearby Baylor University. Pastor Chris Seay visited fraternity and sorority meetings on campus to invite students to worship and within weeks was drawing hundreds of students to Sunday services.

Many ministries are not so ideally situated to tap into college campuses, and certainly many new ministries that attempt to do so may encounter resistance from either established campus ministries or secular college officials. But schools are not the only places of connection. While sociologists have marked the decline of traditional connecting places like business associations, neighborhood groups and churches, most Americans, including Xers, still have wide social networks characterized by what Robert Wuthnow calls in his book by the same name, "loose connections" (Cambridge, Mass.: Harvard University Press, 1998). The stereotypes of Generation Xers as either unemployed slackers or overworked tech-heads ignore that there are, even in the most isolating urban environments, relational networks for churches to tap into. These networks are maintained mostly by informal contact, recreational activities, and mutual interest. Friends keep in touch by e-mail and phone calls more than by formal dinner parties.

In many urban settings, the workplace is the primary social connection for Xers, and corporations in many places have taken the place of the public square by providing cafeterias, fitness facilities, social events, and volunteer opportunities for their employees. Many Gen Xers spend the majority of their waking hours at work, so why not encourage them to see their work as a potential place of ministry and invitation? This is also one of the few places where people of different stages in life—singles, couples without children, parents,

HOW DO THEY KNOW?
ANALYZING INTERNAL COMMUNICATIONS

For each item on the list below, ask yourself the following questions:

1. Are we currently using this means?

2. Does/would it reach a significant portion of our audience?

3. How much initiative and time does it require of the recipient?

4. Does it allow us to communicate with graphics as well as words?

5. Where does it reach people (home, work, while they are already here at church)?

3. Does it allow people to respond quickly and easily to what they read?

4. How much "competition" is there? Will this information get lost in a stack of papers or a list of sixty e-mail messages arriving every day?

Means:

Print newsletter

Weekly bulletin

Brief e-mail messages

E-mail newsletters

Web site newsletter

Bulletin boards

Announcements projected overhead

Personal invitations

Posters/flyers for individual events

Phone tree

and grandparents—interact with a common purpose. Intergenerational congregations have a means of reaching postmodern generations if they can teach their members—of any age—to be witnesses in their workplaces.

Many churches become so focused on mass media forms of communication that they neglect their most powerful tool in communication—the word of mouth of people who have already experienced their congregation. Generation Xers are no different from other generations in at least this respect—they are far more likely to attend a church event because of the invitation of a friend than because of an advertisement, news story, or other impersonal invitation. But even the most enthusiastic participant in a congregation may need reminding that the church exists for "the other." Pastors and evangelism committees need to provide people with tools that make invitation easier. (See "Increasing Word of Mouth Invitation.")

Communicating with a mixed audience

When reaching out to a specific audience—for example, with an outreach that is explicit about being for singles in their twenties, there is a danger in assuming you know the life situation of most of your audience. But even the most narrowly targeted of ministries will have to be conscious of a wide diversity of experiences. Some singles in their twenties have already been through divorce; others may have been sexually abused as children, staying away from intimate relationships of any kind. Others may have come from a traditional, uneventful upbringing by two parents. On a given Sunday morning, a postmodern community might have people struggling with addiction, divorce, depression, economic hardship, and strained family relationships. Their intimate relationships will be affected not only by issues of sex, commitment, and marriage, but also by shifting understandings of sexuality, race, and culture. They may have come from a rigidly pious family or a family with no ties to any faith community or somewhere in-between. They will be in school, between jobs, considering a career change, or underemployed. With such a diverse audience, how can you possibly communicate a single message?

Principle 1. Acknowledge the diversity in your community. You will never be able to touch on every life situation, but postmoderns will appreciate the effort to acknowledge the uniqueness of every situation. And in a community where many people are strangers to one another, the occasional reference to the diversity of life situations (without betraying anyone's confidentiality) can remind the newcomer, "Someone else like me is here too."

Principle 2. Let people's own voices emerge. While one person may take on the primary duty of preaching, pastors need to devise many ways to let people tell their stories in their own ways. This may not always fit into a traditional testimonial style, but the power of the story will more than make up for what a professional may see as technical flaws.

Saint Gregory of Nyssa Episcopal Church in San Francisco holds what most would term a high church liturgy every Sunday, drawing from Orthodox as well as Protestant traditions. But following the sermon, members of the congregation are invited to stand and speak their responses to the word in the style of a Quaker meeting—not to debate a point, but to flesh out the message with experiences from their own lives. The pastors of this congregation admit that this type of speech took a while to enculturate, accustomed as most people are to more adversarial or academic types of discussion, but over time this response time has become a vital part of the community's life.

Principle 3. Teaching should always open up conversation, rather than cut it off. Whereas many Baby Boomer ministries use music, art, and drama to lead in to a linear, spoken message about gospel truth, postmodern ministries may consider the ways in which verbal preaching and teaching are openers to further conversation, rather than an end goal to be communicated. Praxis, a United Methodist coffee house ministry in Minneapolis, Minnesota, offers worship that begins with music and the reading of

INCREASING WORD-OF-MOUTH INVITATION

1. Do we regularly hold events that are geared toward first-time visitors?

2. Do our "regulars" know how to describe accurately what we're about? (Note that this does not necessarily mean knowing the congregation's statement of faith. But members should be prepared to say something more than, "It's cool.")

3. Do we have literature that clearly gives our name, gathering times, and locations? (Many internal forms of communication, like church newsletters, do not regularly include directions to Sunday morning gatherings!)

4. Do we provide members with easy ways to "pass on the word"? Examples include e-mail newsletters, business card-sized invitations, T-shirts, buttons, or other items that invite conversation without demanding a response?

5. Do we encourage nonmembers to invite their friends even if they themselves have not yet committed to the ministry?

Scripture, but which has no traditional preaching per se. Pastor Michelle Hargrave says, "I find I get to do all the proclamationI need toduring the invitation to the table."

Not all postmodern churches throw out the sermon. In fact, many are demonstrating that the myth of thirty-second attention spans is patently false. Mark Driscoll of Mars Hill Church in Seattle preaches forty-five to seventy-five minutes every Sunday. Opportunities for conversation are offered in other ways, such as on a regular radio show and a "theological midrash" page of the community's Web site. A biblical story is introduced on their Web page and callers or visitors to it are encouraged to let the story meet up with their own. Creative biblical interpretation is taught by example and shared by the whole community.

Principle 4. Be prepared to say, "I don't know." Even if you think you have the answer to the problem of God's goodness and the world's evil, be honest about how long and hard Christians have struggled with these issues.

In 1998, politicians across the country were stunned by the election of former pro wrestler Jesse Ventura as governor of Minnesota, and even more astounded by his popular appeal among Gen Xers who had never voted before. Though no one would call him an abjectly humble man, Ventura had one quality that these younger voters found lacking in the traditional candidates: he was willing to say he didn't know instead of giving rhetorical answers. For Gen Xers, an honest shrug is far more trustworthy than a stumbling attempt to appear expert.

Principle 5. Use all of the senses, whenever possible. People from liturgical traditions may want to think creatively about the resources at their disposal for engaging eyes, nose, and bodies in worship as well as the ears. Incense is often used in some rather unlikely places, such as nondenominational churches or churches from a low-church tradition, to welcome worshipers into sacred space. One postmodern coffee house ministry does not include regular preaching in the traditional sense of the word, but instead invites participants to discuss the biblical story and then express its theme in a concrete way, such as the planting of seeds or drawing a picture.

The importance of nonverbal communication is not new to the church; in centuries where literacy was a rare skill, Christians often had to rely on icons, pictures, and rituals to convey the message. While art has been used in the twentieth century to supplement the preached word, some postmodern ministries are starting to see the value of letting art take the lead. House of Mercy, an American

Baptist ministry in the art gallery section of downtown St. Paul, Minnesota, has used liturgical art workshops to teach its members about the Christian story. A "Stations of the Cross" showing of various painters' works during Holy Week drew a crowd of 350 people. Other congregations are learning to pray and worship with icons.

Principle 6. Tell the story early and often. Not every message needs to end with—so Jesus died for us, and so on and so forth. But Generation Xers will resonate most powerfully with the Christian story when it is approached as such—a story that they can enter into. Many postmodern ministries are rediscovering the riches of the Roman Catholic tradition in this regard, teaching the meditation approach called *lectio divina* as a way to hear God's word in Scripture and leading guided meditations as a way of letting the community enter into biblical stories.

Principle 7. Use irony and "edge" appropriately. The Scriptures are full of humor and irony that are frequently lost in our efforts to order them into a seamless system of thought. In both personal and biblical story, don't be afraid to let a little unresolved tension sit. While there is certainly a marked difference between Christian hope and worldly cynicism, it may be appropriate for the preacher to identify with the community instead of the institution at times, in order to demonstrate that one can have doubts, questions, and even anger toward the church without giving up faith in God's ultimate mercy and grace.

Examples of such irony are plentiful in pop culture, where it is commonplace to hear honest social critique expressed in highly satirical forms. The Simpsons TV show, for example, offers a jaded image of the American family and at the same time critiques the shallowness of pop culture itself. Many Christian artists are finding a hearing outside the confines of contemporary Christian recording studios or publishing houses. One example is the writing of Anne Lamott, whose fiction and autobiographical essays are rife with reference to her Christian faith without resorting to pious clichés. Lamott's is a prime example of how brutal honesty—and humor—makes personal testimony more compelling. Describing her attempt to forgive someone, she confesses, "I thought such awful thoughts that I cannot even say them out loud because they would make Jesus want to drink gin straight out of the cat dish" (*Traveling Mercies: Some Thoughts on Faith*, Anne Lamott. New York: Pantheon Books, 1999, p. 131).

Principle 8. Engage pop culture in the service of the gospel. A great deal of popular music, film, and television has conversation about spiritual issues. Certainly, the images that pop culture paints of Christianity and the church are often far from positive, but to ignore the spiritual conversation that holds such a wide audience would be a grave mistake for any postmodern ministry. In 1999, the ministry to Xers that overlooked the newest episode in the *Star Wars* saga missed a huge opportunity! Ministry to Gen Xers continues to let Scripture—though not necessarily the lectionary—set the agenda, but engages pop culture in creative ways to critique the culture as well as to affirm where it is being more honest than the church has often been.

Principle 9. Let the diversity of Scripture stand. Many Xers appreciate that the worldviews of Proverbs and Job, for example, are not entirely consistent. In fact, the apparent contradictions make the Bible more attractive. Rather than trying to smooth over these differences, pastors can demonstrate to Generation Xers how this diversity within Christian Scripture has strengthened the church and allowed for the differences in individual life experience and spiritual growth. While a congregation of Builders and Baby Boomers might prefer to focus on the logical wisdom of Proverbs, postmodern generations will be the first to say, "Yeah, but what about . . . ?" Chris Seay of University Baptist Church in Waco preached extensively on the book of Ecclesiastes in the early days of his congregation and found that the cynicism of this "old man's" book resonated with the college-age congregation.

Principle 10. Be pragmatic in a nonprescriptive way. Generation Xers are an intensely pragmatic people, given to trying out many things to see what works. Although an attempt to teach Xers that Christianity is the truth in propositional terms will probably fail, many Xers will gladly take on spiritual disciplines or acts of servanthood as experiments. Doug Pagitt, formerly of Leadership Network, a Dallas-based organization focused on effective and innovative church leadership, suggests that postmodern ministry might follow the lead of REI, the outdoor sporting goods store that allows customers to try out products of all kinds—from skis to mountain bikes to sleeping bags, right in the store. Churches could likewise see their outreach as "try it on" opportunities for seekers. Offering ways they can be involved in the life of the community without "signing on" will draw them in far more than prescriptive steps to membership.

Using technology

There was a time when "contemporary" church was equated with a sophisticated sound system, presentation software for songs and sermon outlines, and extensive use of video in conveying the message. Many pastors assume that a Web page is the first step to reaching out to younger generations. While a postmodern outreach might use any or all of these means and more, no particular technology is essential, and some may even be a hindrance. The postmodern values of authenticity and spontaneity may in fact argue against the use of some of these technologies. Each community will have to decide for itself. A church in California's Silicon Valley or the Research Triangle of North Carolina may decide that extensive use of the Internet is essential for their internal communications, while an urban church in a working class neighborhood might perceive such efforts as too "corporate."

This said, there are tools available for ministry that can be a great help to hospitality and communication. Xers are far more technologically sophisticated than their parents and generally quite open to the newest, latest trend. Many are so accustomed to e-mail that all of their correspondence takes on its abbreviated, informal style. Some Xers prefer the Web to the mall, and many have found significant others or even spouses through online dating services. As noted earlier, postmodern thinking is far more adaptable to the free-flowing, circular logic of the Web than to linear outlines.

In addition to the way technology may help churches speak the language of postmodern culture, technology properly used also can save money in the long run. E-mail newsletters are cheaper, faster and usually less labor-intensive than the print variety. A Web site can be a helpful, low-risk way for a prospective church visitor to "check it out" (though at the time of this writing it is rarely the place of initial contact with the church). And worship leaders will want to make certain that every visitor can easily hear, see, and participate in a large gathering on Sunday morning. But Xers have lived with faulty software, screeching PAs and slow modems long enough to know that technology is an indifferent ally. The wise leader will take care that these methods are seen as the tools of the whole community to connect with each other, rather than wires and bits that stand between "us" and "them." Decisions about technology will have to be made on a contextual basis, depending upon the current size and goals of the ministry.

GENEROSITY AND HOSPITALITY

Evangelism is ultimately about generosity and hospitality, the natural outgrowth of a desire to share God's gift of grace. Because God is already working in the hearts and minds of postmodern generations, sharing the good news with these generations need not be a program. But no one comes to a party unless he or she receives an invitation, and welcoming unchurched people in the next millennium may require careful rethinking of how your congregation communicates. Just as any good host will consider his or her guests' needs and attitudes in creating a party for them, so a congregation that wants to reach out to postmodern generations will want to consider who they are as saints, sinners, and servants in light of how this generation understands those identities. You will want to look at the gifts God has already given your congregation for outreach, the language unchurched people in your community use to talk about life's problems and challenges, and the best means to identify and welcome those people into your midst. Listen, experiment, invite, and listen again. And in the meantime, keep celebrating. ☩

chapter 4

Worshiping in spirit and truth

Richard Webb

Richard lives in Schaumburg, Illinois, has served as a pastor in Richmond Beach, Washington, and as a regional coordinator for worship and music resources in the Evangelical Lutheran Church in America (ELCA). He currently serves as associate director of evangelism for the ELCA.

What does worship look like for the first generation born in postmodern culture? For University Baptist Church in Waco, Texas, it means worshiping in a dimly lit building that was once a grocery store, then a prosperous megachurch, and currently a stripped-down metal shell—complete with exposed girders, corrugated ceiling panels, and bare hanging light bulbs. The look is intentional. The congregation felt the former worship space was too "Boomer." They wanted something more reflective of their own cultural language and experience.

The stage reflects this same feeling. On either side are two stacked towers of speakers with twenty-five-inch television sets perched on top of each tower. More television sets (vintage 1980s) are spaced around the stage and a large overhead projection screen hangs from the ceiling. During worship these combined forces provide the congregation with words for each song.

Candles are also present—lots of them. In similar congregations, incense is also used, the kind found in university dorms—not what you would find in your typical church! University Baptist is thinking of trying that as well.

So what does worship look like? From Sunday to Sunday in

this setting, worship is never quite the same. In this congregation of more than seven hundred weekly worshipers, variation seems to be the only constant. On one particular Sunday the service began ten minutes after the scheduled time with two ironic and in-your-face announcements, an informal prayer, and a slow meditative congregational song contemplating the healing presence of God. From there the worship tempo slowly began to accelerate like a train pulling out of the station until it pulsed with the power and energy of a live Pearl Jam concert. The music ranged from an edgy alternative style that sounded like the Dave Matthews Band to early American hymns with a strong Scottish accent, almost all of it written or arranged by the congregation's musicians.

After twenty-five minutes of singing, informal prayer, and several short reflections on Scripture, one of University Baptist's many lay leaders, a deacon about twenty-five years old, delivered a lively talk on Mark 12:41-44, the story of the widow and the two coins. Towards the end of his forty-minute reflection he gave the congregation a homework assignment to help them apply what they had learned. The ninety-minute service concluded with one more song, an offering, an image meditation, more announcements, and a final prayer.

University Baptist is one example of how congregations across North America have made the decision to speak the language of Generation X in their worship services. Throughout the U.S. and Canada, local churches are once again discovering what they learned with other ethnic and generational cohorts: the gospel must be contextualized for each new community of believers.

WORSHIP IN POSTMODERN TIMES

What does this example tell us about worship with the first generation of postmodern culture? For one thing, it signals a profound change in the way many Christian communities organize their worship life. In this community and many like it, the worship service and even the worship space are considered to be faithful to the extent they express not only the story of God's truth and love, but also the story of the gathered community.

That means one size no longer fits all. Some congregations seem to invent their forms from scratch while others borrow significantly from traditional sources. The Generation X community at Forest Hill Church in Charlotte, North Carolina often employs traditional litanies in its worship. Mars Hill Fellowship in Seattle frequently uses ancient prayers and creeds in its services. On the other hand, worship leaders and preachers at University Baptist tend to improvise their way through Sunday morning, following what they sense to be the prompting of God's Spirit.

In her book *Worship Evangelism*, Sally Morgenthaler observes that no single worship pattern or style characterizes Christian worship within Generation X culture. She notes that while the approach of each of the three churches she interviewed seemed to be effective for its context, each also has its own worship format (*Worship Evangelism: Inviting Unbelievers into the Presence of God*, Sally Morgenthaler. Grand Rapids, Mich.: Zondervan, 1995).

In typical postmodern fashion, for Protestant congregations that serve and are led by the Generation X community, radical contextualization seems to be the only commonality. But while the particular worship expression of each congregation may be unique, there still seem to be some key characteristics that permeate the strategies of most of their worship services. Here are nine of the most apparent.

Focusing on God

Worship geared for Boomers has been occasionally, and somewhat unfairly, criticized for being overly focused on the needs of the worshiper. This is hardly the case with congregations that reach out effectively to the Generation X community. Typically these worshiping communities are fiercely committed to God being the center of everything that happens in worship. They believe that the most important things a worshiper can experience are Jesus' truth and love. For them the issue of contextualization starts not with meeting the needs of the worshiper, rather with the clear proclamation of the gospel. Many of these young leaders themselves have only recently been touched by the power of this gospel and they deeply desire to share this experience with their friends. In this way they stand with the sixteenth-century church reformers who understood worship as an event of God's word.

The use of bricolage

In his book, *Virtual Faith*, Tom Beaudoin defines bricolage as "an improvised, rough assemblage of whatever tools are at hand to solve a problem" (*Virtual Faith: The Irreverent Spiritual Quest of Generation X*, Tom Beaudoin. San Francisco, Calif.: Jossey Bass, 1996, p. 149). He goes on to say that this is characteristic of the way Generation Xers are building their culture: by taking diverse and often contradictory elements from existing cultural traditions and recombining them to form the building blocks of their own emerging traditions.

The same thing is happening in their churches. In congregations where Generation Xers worship, it is not uncommon to find a wide range of music and ritual styles all mixed together to form something new and uniquely expressive of their own community. At a Leadership Network conference for young church leaders, the closing service of Holy Communion involved elements of Roman Catholic, Lutheran, Calvinist, Baptist, and Charismatic traditions.

Darkness, incense, and candles greeted the worshipers as they entered the sanctuary. The first two acts of worship were meditation and confession. By contrast, the music sung during the distribution of the bread, wine, and grape juice was a wild, high-energy mixture of alternative, world music, and rock opera, styles characteristic of this generation. Participants were dancing in the pews. Even the overhead screen displayed the influence of bricolage. When not used to lead songs, it illuminated the room with icons and paintings of the crucifixion. The juxtapositions that occur in bricolage were heightened by the fact that the two presiding ministers were a Southern Baptist and a nondenominational pastor.

Indigenous worship strategies

If bricolage is characteristic of churches where Generation Xers worship, it should come as no surprise that these congregations are also known for their uniquely indigenous worship styles. For them, faithful and effective worship springs in part from the cultural language and experience of both the worshiping community and those God has called them to reach. This affects ritual form, music, artwork, preaching styles, and all other possible components of their worship.

One of the obvious consequences of this emphasis is the radical diversity of musical styles evident among congregations thriving in this context. The worship music at Spirit Garage, a Lutheran congregation in Minneapolis, sounds a lot like blues and classic rock 'n' roll. By contrast, the worship band at Pathways Church in the Denver area leads the congregation primarily with rhythm and blues and fusion jazz, music styles more traditionally associated with Boomer tastes. At University Baptist, the music divides up into two basic streams: Appalachian folk music and music reminiscent of the hypnotic rhythms and harmonies of the Dave Matthews Band.

A frustrating byproduct for worship leaders in other congregations is the fact that very little of this music has been published. With local churches in the Generation X community writing most of their own music, there has been almost nothing mass-produced until recently.

The radical diversity of preaching styles among Generation X congregations also demonstrates the trend toward contextualization. Pastor Mark Driscoll of Mars Hill Fellowship preaches weighty one-hour expository-type sermons. By contrast, Pastor Pam Fickenscher of Spirit Garage, gives talks that connect Sunday's Bible readings with situations from everyday life. On occasion, Chris Seay, the lead pastor of University Baptist, will divide his informal sermons into several bite-sized components, sprinkled throughout the service. At each of these congregations, worshipers remark that the preachers seem to be preaching straight at them and into their life situations. One of the things all three preachers all hold in common is that they preach in narrative fashion. In their sermons they strive to connect the story of Jesus to the stories of the hearers. This is a departure from the popular preaching style of the past few decades, which is seminar-style sermons based more on ideas than stories.

The postmodern cultural tendency toward contextualization contrasts sharply with the worship practices of the last two centuries. Until recently, much of North American worship life has been characterized by a momentum toward uniformity. Among some Lutherans, colonial pastor Henry Melchior Muhlenberg's dream of one common hymnal in North America was viewed by many as practically inspired. Other denominations have had similar visions for their worshiping communities. Even among congregations that have reached out effectively to Boomers, their music comes mostly out of three main publishing houses: Maranatha!, Hosanna! Music, and Vineyard publishing.

Multisensate experience

Generation Xers grew up in the midst of a radical shift in the way people learned and made sense of experience. Among adults alive today, generations prior to Generation X made sense of life linearly, processing one experience or solving one problem at a time. The book was both the primary medium and metaphor for this way of thinking. The new "books" for Generation X have become the video game and the Internet. In both cases Xers experience a multitude of rapid and simultaneous bursts of information in an interactive manner. These recent forms of electronic media have trained this generation in radically new ways of learning and problem solving.

The ramifications for worship are enormous. In order to

engage this techno-savvy generation with the gospel, worship in many congregations has become heavily multisensate. At any given time during worship, several simultaneous and diverse types of experience may be involved. Of course, this goes far beyond the use of multimedia technology. Ordinary items such as candles, tapestries, paintings, dance, and drama also enhance the worship experience.

But multisensate worship experiences are not just about multi-sensory input; they involve the active participation of the worshiper in as many ways as possible, such as spontaneous congregational dance, interactive sermons, and small-group prayer. Multisensate worship means that the way the word is proclaimed must ignite the imagination in as many ways as possible.

Postliterate environment

If worship for the Generation X community is multisensate, it follows that it also postliterate. That means effective worship forms within this context must take into account that the primary learning venue for Xers is no longer the book. This does not mean that Xers don't or won't read. It simply means that this generation does most of its learning and communicating through vehicles other than the static printed page.

As a result, most worship practices in this community are orally-oriented and make heavy use of informal prayers, conversational sermons, and so forth. This has profound implications for worship traditions that rely heavily on scripted forms such as printed prayers, dialogues, and litanies. Denominations such as Lutherans and Episcopalians will be challenged to move beyond their hymnals and prayer books as their primary vehicles for worship. In many ways, they will be pushed to develop orally-oriented worship forms similar to the liturgical traditions of the denominations more indigenous to North American culture. Anticipating this change, the worship strategies of Vatican II radically reduced the amount of "scripting" found in the Roman

Catholic mass. Catholic liturgical tradition now relies on the printed page almost as little as the Evangelical tradition does.

Nonlinear worship patterns

The nonlinear experiences provided by the Internet and video games have also influenced the way Xers organize their worship patterns. Traditional and Boomer services often have a set pattern that begins with praise and adoration, moves to the word of God, continues with the celebration of the Lord's Supper, and then concludes by sending worshipers out into the world for witness and service. While the priorities of these elements are affirmed, congregations that serve Generation X communities will often mix these elements up and/or spread them throughout the service.

One worship service at Mars Hill Fellowship began with silence, then a single song of confession, which then moved straight into an hour-long message. After the message the congregation sang songs of praise and adoration for more than thirty minutes. Another service began and concluded with about twenty minutes of highly energetic praise music where many worshipers danced and lifted their hands in the air. As mentioned earlier, a common practice at University Baptist is to comingle elements of praise, confession, and meditation with elements of the sermon.

A sense of mystery

Every Sunday night at 9:30 P.M. more than one thousand young adults gather for worship at St. Mark's Episcopal Cathedral in Seattle. What attracts them to a church service at such an odd time? An incredible rock band? A high-tech multimedia presentation? Quite the opposite. These Gen Xers are attending the ancient evening service of Compline, straight from the Book of Common Prayer. Every Sunday evening a men's choir chants this century-old rite in a darkened cathedral so full of people that many are forced to sit in the aisles and on the steps of the altar.

Even where worship is less traditional, where the music is more reflective of contemporary culture, congregations often employ ancient prayers, creeds, art, and music along with their sound systems and LCD projectors (overhead projection operated via lap-top computer). Many of these congregations worship in partial darkness, illuminated only by candles on the stage and the light of the overhead screen. Mars Hill Fellowship in Seattle often begins its worship in total silence.

But this desire for mystery goes beyond old cathedrals, candles, and darkness. Xer worshipers live in a complex and ambiguous world where there are few clear answers and even fewer clear choices. They don't want to hear about "five steps" to this or that spiritual goal. Frankly, they don't want to hear about "five steps" to anything! Their world doesn't work that way. Their world is one of mystery, chaos, and unanswerable questions. What they want is preaching that dares to dive into reality. They want someone to take notice of the gray and help them deal with the hard choices of their daily lives.

Telling the truth

While Generation Xers desire mystery, they also want someone finally to tell the truth about things. Many Xers grew up in family, neighborhood, and cultural situations where pain and chaos were the norm. In *13th Gen*, authors Neil Howe and Bill Strauss note that half of this cohort was raised in nontraditional families (usually the result of divorce), another half experienced physical or sexual abuse at the hands of a family member or close relative, and nearly all of them were "virtual orphans." For many of them as they grew up, their parents simply were not around. The term "latchkey kid" applied to many of them when they were children. Furthermore, this was the first generation to be taught by their schools and by the scandals of the last two decades that there really was no truth beyond the subjectiveness of personal experience and desires of the powerful.

For them it seemed that everything was up for grabs. There was no firm footing of any kind. Not rational, not relational. For that reason Xers have a particular craving for some kind of bedrock, some kind of ground to stand on in the midst of all the craziness.

Xers want worship that's real. They can get entertainment at the movies or with video games. They want to be told the truth—about the brokenness of their families, their friends, their culture, and their own lives. They want an honest prognosis of the future, even if it isn't pretty. For that reason effective preaching in the Generation X context is particularly blunt and to the point. It reaches right into the pain of their lives, comforts, critiques, and points to another way.

Stories over ideas

Another shift in culture involves the move from idea to story as the primary conveyer of reality. For previous generations influenced by modern thought, effective sermons usually involve a business seminar presentation of a series of concrete and logical points, which leads to an irrefutable conclusion. Not so with the first generation of postmodern culture. The most powerful presentation of the gospel is bound up in the story of Jesus and the stories of changed lives.

That means preaching must be narrative in character. Indeed, some would suggest that the entire worship experience must have the feel and flow of a story. This is particularly the case with congregations that plan their worship services on a given theme. Ginghamsburg United Methodist Church, near Tipp City, Ohio, will go so far as to arrange the stage of its worship space to coordinate with the theme of that Sunday's music and the preaching.

KNOWING THE BOTTOM LINE

There appears to be no end to the dizzying array of worship styles and patterns found in congregations where Generation Xers gather. Nevertheless, there are some key characteristics implicit in most of the strategies and practices used by these worshiping communities. But while these characteristics give us a glimpse into the context and values of these worshiping communities, they are not enough to provide us with an adequate foundation for making sound decisions about worship. If we desire to proclaim the gospel to unchurched and dechurched Xers with any confidence that it is indeed the gospel we are proclaiming, we need to base our strategies on something beyond the commonalities of the present practices.

So, as we examine worship in this emerging context, what criteria will help us develop ways to plan and lead worship that are at once faithful to the truth of the gospel and effective in touching lives with the saving and healing presence of Jesus? There are three places for reflection that can provide us with the criteria we need to help us plan faithful and effective worship services:

- The Scriptures
- The experience of the worshiper
- The worship strategies of the reformers

The Scriptures ground us in the story of God's dealings with humanity. They reveal to us the pattern and purpose of God's revelation in human experience and what that might mean for faithful and effective worship practice. Examining the experience of the worshiper helps us look for appropriate parallels between humanity's experience of God in the Scriptures and our experience of God in worship. Finally, reflection on the worship strategies of the reformers gives us a glimpse into how they grappled with these same issues as they sought to define anew the purpose of the church.

Worship and the Scriptures

As we make our way through the stories of the Bible, we find that a general pattern emerges in the way God deals with individual people. The vision of the prophet Isaiah illustrates this well:

> In the year that King Uzziah died, I saw the Lord sitting on a throne, high and lofty; and the hem of his robe filled the temple. Seraphs were in attendance above him; each had six wings: with

two they covered their faces, and with two they covered their feet, and with two they flew. And one called to another and said:

"Holy, holy, holy is the LORD of hosts;

the whole earth is full of his glory."

The pivots on the thresholds shook at the voices of those who called, and the house filled with smoke. And I said: "Woe is me! I am lost, for I am a man of unclean lips, and I live among a people of unclean lips; yet my eyes have seen the King, the LORD of hosts!" Then one of the seraphs flew to me, holding a live coal that had been taken from the altar with a pair of tongs. The seraph touched my mouth with it and said: "Now that this has touched your lips, your guilt has departed and your sin is blotted out." Then I heard the voice of the Lord saying, "Whom shall I send, and who will go for us?" And I said, "Here am I; send me!" (Isaiah 6:1-8).

What does this passage tell us about Isaiah's experience of God?

God's overwhelming presence. Isaiah encountered a God whose presence and power is infinite and thus cannot be contained by the limitations of the national shrine. The Seraphs announced that "the whole earth is full of his glory" (Isaiah 6:3). Only the hem of God's robe could occupy the temple. Indeed, the Seraphs' message alone was enough to rattle the temple thresholds, along with its implicit promises of security, control, and permanence. Furthermore, this God is called "holy," one whose character and power lie far beyond our ability to imagine. This is the God who shatters the "truths" of our sinful vested interests and confronts us instead with terrifying reality.

God's truth. Whatever illusions Isaiah had built up regarding himself and his people were shattered by the truth of God's presence. Isaiah took upon himself the ritual word of mourning for the dead ("woe") because he saw himself and his community for who they really were, a broken people in rebellion against a sovereign God (v. 5).

God's forgiveness. Fortunately this frightening truth was not the last word. Instead one of the Seraphs took a burning coal from the altar, a place of forgiveness and reconciliation, and proclaimed to Isaiah that he was free from his sin and guilt. From the burning coal we learn that God's means of grace is sometimes a violent one. For Isaiah the moment of terror became one and the same with the moment of life.

God's call to proclaim the Word. Here the purpose of Isaiah's vision is revealed. The point is not the religious experience; the point is what comes afterwards. The revelation of God's presence, truth, and forgiveness all drive toward Isaiah's call to action. An encounter with God's presence means an involvement with God's mission.

In one way or another, this fourfold pattern permeates the entirety of Scripture. For that reason theologians refer to this story and others like it (Abraham and Sarah, Jeremiah, Mary, Paul) as a "call account." In every account, it is God who initiates the encounter and almost everyone finds the experience overwhelming. It is no accident that the most often used phrase by the angels in Luke's Gospel is "fear not."

God's presence also reveals the truth of our situation, be it our sin (Isaiah) or simply the inability to respond to the task to which we are called (a virgin bearing a child). But there is always some kind of burning coal. With the apostle Paul, it was the healing of his vision—in more ways than one! With Mary it was the assurance of God's power. With Moses it was the strange grace of God's motivating anger. Finally everyone is given a task: Tell the Gentiles about my love (Acts 9:15). You shall lead my people out of Egypt (Exodus 3:10). "You will bear a son" (Luke 1:31). "Go make disciples of all nations" (Matthew 28:19).

Even—perhaps particularly—in the story of Jesus this pattern is borne out. The story begins with God making the first move. Jesus is born to Mary not out of human initiative, but through divine will. The angel announces to Mary God's break-in into the closed universe of human experience and concludes with the words: "for nothing will be impossible with God" (Luke 1:37).

Thirty years later this bewildering Rabbi Jesus tells his disciples, "You did not choose me but I chose you" (John 15:16).

Throughout Jesus' ministry, we see a constant interplay between the disciples' brokenness and blindness and the red-hot coal of Jesus' love and truth. And all for the purpose of calling them into God's great life-saving love and mission for them.

Examining the experience of the worshiper

In the latter part of the twentieth century, Edward Demming, a statistician by profession, caused a stir among production and quality control experts by suggesting a new way to define quality in industrial production. He proposed that businesses stop defining the quality of their products from the standpoint of their production specifications and instead define them from the standpoint of the customer's experience. In other words, if the customer is satisfied, the producers had a quality product. Initially ignored by North American corporations, Demming took his proposal to Japan where the Japanese business community made it the foundation of what became one of the world's most powerful economies.

While Demming's proposal doesn't quite work for evaluating Christian worship services, he still has a point. What would it mean if we evaluated the faithfulness and effectiveness of our worship services from the standpoint of what God desired worshipers to experience? It would mean first of all focusing less on what we *do* in worship and more on what the worshiper *experiences.* It would then mean making our decisions about worship content and style on the basis of that perspective.

Let's apply this principle to the way God is revealed to individuals in Scripture. If the four-fold pattern of Isaiah's vision is typical of how God connects with people throughout the Bible, what might that mean in terms of how God intends to connect with people in our worship services? We can say that worshipers should experience:

- God's powerful presence;
- God's illusion-shattering truth;
- God's forgiveness, healing, and salvation through Jesus Christ;
- God's irresistible call to bring this saving word to others.

From this perspective, if, as in the past, we are primarily concerned about whether we use a praise band or a pipe organ, whether we worship in a cathedral or a warehouse, or whether we use hymnals or overhead screens, we have missed the point. All of these activities may assist us in creating an effective worship environment, but focusing on them will not tell us if our worship has been effective in revealing God's power, truth, salvation, and call to the worshiper. For that we need to ask the worshiper.

Cross-cultural missionaries also discovered this principle. Wycliffe Bible Translators is an organization dedicated to translating the Bible into every language on the planet. When a member of that organization encounters a new culture for the first time he or she begins his or her task by listening closely to the language, values, and traditions of this new culture. Then, in partnership with members of this culture, the missionary begins to translate the Bible. Throughout this process the members of the host culture are asked to provide constant feedback in regard to the accuracy of the translation. The point is that these missionaries cannot do their jobs without paying attention to the experience of those whom they serve.

So how do we evaluate our worship practices from the experience of the worshiper? To accomplish this, Eastside Foursquare in north suburban Seattle assembled a weekly worship evaluation team. The first action of the team was to design a set of questions that would help them discover what worshipers experienced in their services. Then, every week, at the close of their services, the team surveyed several randomly chosen worshipers as they left the worship space. This information was then given to the pastors and worship leaders for weekly review at their staff meetings. More

115

than forty years ago, Demming proposed this practice to the business community. He called it "constant evaluation" and felt it would keep corporate structures and strategies from stagnating.

Another congregation, Ascension Lutheran Church in Waukesha, Wisconsin, evaluated their worship services with the aid of a focus group consisting of unchurched people from their neighborhood. The leadership of Ascension made a promise to the group that they would be asked to attend worship only one time. After the group had attended the services, the staff brought them together to ask them what they experienced. Next they asked the group what kind of worship service they would truly want to attend and to which they would most likely invite their friends. This information helped them design a seeker-friendly worship service where worshipers now fill every seat in the house.

Worship and the Reformation tradition

During the Protestant Reformation, Martin Luther and John Calvin also wrestled with questions regarding worship in their contexts. They were confronted with a medieval church, which taught that if the ritual of the Mass was performed correctly according to certain rules, then the appropriate divine outpouring of grace ensued. Essentially worship was about performing certain ritual formulae. The experience of the worshiper really had nothing to do with it. In fact, a valid medieval Mass required only the presence of its performer, the priest.

For the reformers, the rediscovery of God's free and unlimited gift of grace left no room for the medieval way of thinking about worship. Free grace meant that there was no need to conjure anything up. Hence new ways of talking about worship were required. How would we talk about and practice worship in a way that takes into account the unconditional nature of God's grace?

Notwithstanding certain differences, both Calvin and Luther responded by asserting that biblical worship is not about ritual formulae, but about the mediation of God's presence through the proclamation of God's word. In the emerging Reformation tradition, while ritual still played a major role, it no longer was at the center of the equation. The Lutheran reformers expressed this new understanding of worship through article seven of the Augsburg Confession: "The church is the assembly of saints in which the gospel is taught purely and the sacraments are administered rightly" (The Book of Concord, Fortress Press, 1959, p. 32).

Luther articulated this further through three key principles that he felt were necessary for the faithful interpretation of Scripture. These work equally well as ways to unpack the Reformation understanding of worship. They are:

- The four solas: Christ alone, Scripture alone, grace alone, faith alone;
- The proclamation categories of law and gospel;
- The means of grace: Word and Sacrament.

In other words, worship that is faithful to the gospel leads the worshiper to experience:

- Christ alone as the source of all hope and salvation;
- Scripture alone as the place where we learn about this gracious Messiah;
- God's grace alone through which hope and salvation are offered;
- Faith alone as the way we receive God's gracious gift.

The worshiper discovers these four solas through the proclamation of law and gospel. Law: God's commands colliding with our rebellion and the illusions we have about, ourselves, God, and our neighbor. We are exposed as the broken people we truly are. Gospel: The free gift of Jesus' life, death, and resurrection that overcomes our brokenness with his eternal life for us.

This good news takes its shape through Word and Sacrament. Word: The experience of God's presence through the proclamation of the law and the gospel. Sacraments: For Lutherans, the experience of God's presence in baptism and the Lord's Supper.

Thus, at the heart of the Augsburg Confession, as well as Luther's key principles, stands the assertion that worship is an event of the gospel. Its primary purpose is to lead the worshiper to experience what God has done in Jesus. In that same vein, Lutheran and Calvinist reformers reconnected the power of the sacraments back to the proclamation of the gospel rather than to the authority of a divine institution and its sanctioned ritual actions.

Since, according to these reformers, ritual action did not carry with it any inherent divine grace, they began to see worship ritual primarily as a vehicle of communication for the proclamation of the gospel as well as a way to join the experience of the individual worshiper into the experience of the worshiping community. This new understanding of worship gave rise to the contextual strategies reflected in the early worship services of the Lutheran tradition. Article seven of the Augsburg Confession reflects this shift when it states that "It is not necessary that human traditions or rites and ceremonies, instituted by [people], should be alike everywhere. It is as Paul says, 'One faith, one baptism, one God and Father of all,' (Ephesians 4:5-6)" (*The Book of Concord*, Fortress Press, 1959, p. 32).

In Luther's case he felt this could be accomplished by designing worship strategies that contextualized the four basic actions of the Mass:

• Gathering together in praise and preparation;

• Hearing the word of God;

• Feasting on the word through the meal of the Lord's Supper;

• Being sent out into the world to make Christ known.

The first of these contextual worship strategies was the Formula Missae or Order of Public Worship, a service in Latin designed to proclaim the gospel to educated urban Germans. Ironically many contemporary Lutherans would now find this worship service to be "too Catholic." The liturgy remained in Latin; the presider still wore all the traditional vestments of the medieval Catholic church; and candles and incense were still in abundance. But that was, after all, the "soul language" of those the Formula Missae intended to reach.

By contrast, Luther later published a service that came to be known as the Deutsche Messe, or German Mass. This service was designed for use in rural and urban and working-class communities. It emphasized the use of vernacular language, simple ritual forms, and popular music (or worship music written in popular style). Donald Grout, in *A History of Western Music*, sites one of the most famous examples of this appropriation strategy: the bawdy secular song "Mein Gemüth ist mir verwirret" (*A History of Western Music*, Donald Jay Grout. New York: W.W. Norton and Co., Inc., p. 253, 1996). The first four lines of the original text are as follows:

> My soul is all bewildered—
> A maiden's tender charms!
> How great is my confusion;
> There's sickness my heart.
>
> —ENGLISH TRANSLATION, RICHARD WEBB

English worshipers know this tune as the great Reformation hymn "O Sacred Head Now Wounded." Luther and his colleagues felt free to appropriate music from a variety of unlikely sources, as long as it effectively served to proclaim the gospel with purity and with clarity.

Early Lutheran worship practices challenge present day congregations to discover and employ the ritual and musical languages of the Generation X community. Depending upon the local context, this will mean different things for different settings. Some congregations will make extensive use of house music and urban rock. Others might use garage band ska and acid jazz, styles utterly foreign to most readers of this book (but you need to be open to learning about them). Still others might employ a mixture of Gregorian Chant, American folk hymnody, and alternative music. The possibilities are endless. Whatever the solution, effective worship strategies will need to be organic to the communities they serve.

DEVELOPING CRITERIA

From this reflection on Scripture, Reformation worship practices, and the experience of the worshiper, we now can explore some statements about worship that can help congregational leaders make decisions that will move them toward faithful and effective worship strategies and practices for this generation.

God's presence

Worship is where we discover God's presence. Worship is not some kind of event that we manipulate to deliver a religious experience. It is not a religious version of the traveling medicine show. Isaiah's vision reminds us that, if anything, worship is a place where we discover the God who has been with us all along. "Listen! I am standing at the door, knocking" (Revelation 3:20). Our job as worship leaders is to play the role of John the Baptist and make the way straight for the coming of the Lord.

God's power

Worship is where we discover God's power. Scripture points out that whenever God shows up in human affairs, people experience strong emotion. At the sight of God, Isaiah thought he would die. When the two Marys heard the angel's message of Jesus' resurrection, they ran and hid. In *Teaching a Stone to Talk*, Annie Dillard wrote concerning worship that "It is madness to wear ladies' straw hats and velvet hats to church; we should all be wearing crash helmets. Ushers should issue life preservers and signal flares; they should lash us to our pews. For the sleeping god may wake someday and take offense, or the waking god may draw us out to where we can never return (*Teaching a Stone to Talk*, Annie Dillard. New York: HarperPerennial, 1982).

God's truth

Worship is where we discover God's truth. While our God is a joyous God who calls us to celebrate what Jesus has done for us, God also calls us to face the truth of our brokenness and the brokenness of the world around us. The stories of Scripture indicate over and over that the revelation of God's presence is also a revelation of God's truth. Both theologically and in the context of the Generation X community, anything less than the straight story will not work.

What Jesus has done

Worship is where we discover what Jesus has done for us. For Lutheran reformers and many others today, worship is about the proclamation of the gospel. That means that worship is not a self-help course, nor is it about the cause-of-the-month. Christian worship is about the only hope for humanity, Jesus the Messiah.

Experience

Worship must be evaluated from the experience of the worshiper. In many ways, worship is an event of communication. For this reason it is of paramount importance that we ask the worshiper what he or she heard when the gospel was proclaimed through ritual, music, preaching, and the administration of the sacraments.

Context

Worship must speak into the context of the worshiper. If our worship strategies are going to be shaped by the experience of the worshiping community, they will be shaped by the context of that community as well. If the worship strategies of the Reformation tradition teach us anything, it is that faithful worship is also contextual worship.

Contextualization will pose a tremendous challenge for congregations that believe that all of their members should worship the same way. Because of larger cultural shifts (the move from modernity to postmodernity in Western culture), the gap between younger generations and older generations is growing wider. This is not because Generation Xers are hostile to other generations—quite the opposite. With the exception of some Boomer traditions, this community is open to employing the traditions and language of as many generational and ethnic groups as possible. That is what bricolage is all about.

The problem usually lies with other generations. Do the parents and grandparents of Xers really want to praise God with a mixture of loud alternative, urban rock, ska, and Celtic folk music? Do they really want to worship in a dimly-lit warehouse (or even their own worship space) filled with the smoke of incense and illuminated only by candles and an overhead screen?

The issue is not about who welcomes whom. It's about the experience of worship connecting to the context of the worshipers. Sometimes the differences are just too great for intergenerational worship strategies. It would be like insisting that immigrant Hmong and Guatemalan communities worship every Sunday in one blended service. It just won't work. They want to worship in a language they understand. That's why the congregations that are most effective at reaching into the Generation X community provide worship specifically in the cultural language of that community.

DEVELOPING STRATEGIES

The six criteria above not only help to describe worship that is faithful and effective but also serve as criteria from which leaders can test their strategies for worship in the Generation X community. So now what is the next move? How do you move from reflection to action? Below are some key steps you'll need to take as your congregation makes plans for worship within the context of the Generation X community. At the end of this chapter you will find worksheets to assist you in your planning.

Listening to your context

We have already seen that one of the hallmarks of Generation X culture is its extreme diversity. Particularly in worship, there is no such thing as a Generation X style of music or ritual. There is no plug and-play worship strategy that will automatically cause scores of Xers to flood into our congregations. Those seeking to do faithful and effective worship within this community will need to listen very carefully to Xer musical and ritual languages. Here are some ways you can listen in to the context of your community.

Spend time with the people God has called you to reach. One congregation called together all the inactive Xers of its congregation and met with them over pizza for about ninety minutes. Congregational leaders engaged the focus group in frank discussion about the kind of ritual, music, and message that would be meaningful to them in a worship service.

In addition to one-on-one conversation you can take a snapshot of the Generation X community in your area through statistical demographics. Often you can get this information from denominational offices, the local chamber of commerce, local governments, and school districts. Be careful not to use this information as your only basis for decisions. Overreliance on statistical information can mislead you as to the real nature of your local community.

Visit the music stores in your community and ask the sales staff which compact discs and audiocassettes are most popular with the Xers who frequent their stores. Purchase several representative pieces of music and spend some time listening to them. Studying the lyrics will give you a window into the hopes, fears, and values of these listeners.

Attend local performance events popular with the Generation X community. These might be large-scale events at arenas or stadiums or smaller events taking place at bars or coffee houses. This also will give you an opportunity to see how Generation Xers interact with each other.

Church consultant Bill Easum suggests that congregations do a survey of their local radio stations to find out which ones charge the most for commercial advertisements. Higher advertising fees indicate a larger share of the targeted audience. So it will also be important to ask these stations which generational groups fit their target market.

Evaluate the faithfulness and effectiveness of your present practices. Discover how both members and guests alike experience your worship services. Strategies like the ones used at Eastside Foursquare in Seattle and Ascension Lutheran in Waukesha can be helpful for this task.

Chances are, the ones doing this research may not be the ones who plan and lead the worship that serves the Generation X community. Not to worry. The primary purpose of "listening in" to their music and culture is to help your congregation understand both the needs and context this service will be addressing. It will also help your congregation be aware of the kind of music leadership this service will require.

Gathering worship leadership

One of the points of frustration for church leaders is that it is difficult to plan and lead worship in the Generation X community if you are not part of that community. Their musical and ritual languages are so distinct from any other generation's that it is diffi-cult to make the linguistic jump necessary for effective communi-cation. Thus, part of your listening process will involve discerning where there are Generation Xers who might be called to be part of the music leadership team. This also applies to areas such as preach-ing and presiding. In most cases it is desirable to have leaders from the Generation X community fill these positions as well. Here are some steps you can take to help you discover these leaders.

Look for Xer musicians who have a passion for reaching their generation with Jesus' saving love. While musical competence is very important, it is the passion for those who don't know Jesus that is key to this ministry. If your musician has an evangelist's passion it will also help him or her keep the music in balance with the rest of the worship.

You and your congregation will need to commit to serious and intentional prayer. Since many of the Generation X community are not actively a part of a congregation or the church, finding a leader for your music team could be difficult. You will need the confidence that God is in charge of the journey.

Look first for musicians in your congregation. Again, be patient while you search. It may take a little time. Because their brand of music has not always been greeted enthusiastically by other generations, Xer musicians are often not very eager to be in the spotlight.

If there are no potential leaders for the music team in your congregation you might try the following places:

Local colleges. Usually there is either a college paper or bulletin board in the music building for want ads. When you post your ad, be clear that you are looking for a musician interested in leading worship.

Music stores. Try networking with the sales clerks as well as post-ing your position on their bulletin boards.

City newspapers and local trade magazines. These sources will give you access to professional musicians. Again, in your ads remember to make it clear that you are looking for a musician to lead worship.

Network with music leaders of large churches involved in similar ministries. Often these people will know someone who knows someone. This is actually a very fruitful source.

Neighboring megachurches with an overflow of musicians. Extremely large congregations that use contemporary music often attract an overflow of high-quality musicians.

Bars and coffeehouses where the Generation X community gathers. Often you can find excellent Christian musicians performing at bars because their churches don't like their music! Many of them are waiting for the chance to use their music within a congregational ministry setting.

Training worship leaders

If you're not from the Generation X community, you may have difficulty training your music team leaders on the finer points of hip hop or ska. But you can meet with them regularly to pray, study, and help them think strategically about worship. This will be particularly important if your music team leaders are not familiar with your denomination's particular perspective on worship. Below are some steps you can take to provide training for your leaders.

• Support them financially so that they can take advantage of continuing education opportunities. In fact, pay them enough so that they have the freedom of time to develop their craft.

• Encourage them to network with other music team leaders who are in similar ministry settings. If your congregation has the resources, you may want to host monthly network gatherings for fellowship and exchange of ideas.

• Have a regular Bible study with your music leaders where together you examine the Scriptures for principles and models of worship.

• Walk through your denomination's perspective on worship

with them and explain to them the nonnegotiables (be certain beforehand that they really are nonnegotiable). Let them know where the boundaries are before they run into them by accident.

• Help them develop habits of worshiper-oriented planning and constant evaluation. Remind them now and then of the over-all biblical goals of the service. Let them know that you're available to walk together with them through any challenge that may arise.

• Be their advocate to the congregation and its leadership. As with any change or innovation, there will be conflict and often it's the musicians who get caught in the crossfire. Let your music team know that you will back their play.

Planning your worship service

The following are areas you and your leadership team will need to consider as you plan worship for this service. Except in rare cases, if you are not a part of the Generation X community, consider giving this area over to Gen X leadership. As members of the community the congregation is called to serve, they will be best equipped in terms of how to proceed.

You will, however, need to be aware of the areas listed below and the challenges and opportunities they present in terms of advocacy, prayer support, financial planning, and overall guidance.

Worship time. Congregations within the Generation X community worship at every time imaginable. Many of them worship at night. The lifestyle patterns of your community will determine which time makes sense for your strategy.

Worship space. Some postmodern congregations worship in barren spaces such as warehouses and gyms. Others gather in stately old cathedral-like buildings. Whatever the shape of the space, this community tends to view their places of worship more as tabernacles than as temples. Thus, they tend to define their spaces more by their own artwork and ritual action than through the architecture of the building.

Ritual style. At least two things come into play: the formality of worship that conveys a sense of mystery and the orality of worship in a postliterate and multisensate environment. This refers to the change we're experiencing more and more in communication in our culture—it goes beyond the written word and printed page; it engages several senses simultaneously. This will be a source of tension for worship leaders as they plan worship. In order to keep things in balance, they will need to be aware of how the community experiences the services they lead.

Preaching style. As earlier illustrations in this chapter have demonstrated, there is a diversity of preaching styles used in the Generation X community, each dependent upon its particular context. The important thing for this community is that preaching needs to speak clearly and truthfully about the ambiguities of experience, about the brokenness of life, and about the hope that Jesus offers us.

Music style. This is a basic communication issue. Whatever the style of music employed, it needs to connect with the experience of the worshiper. For that reason, most musicians in effective Generation X congregations write their own music. They are singing the story of God in their communities. In some congregations, it simply isn't possible for the musicians to write their own music. The resources at the end of this book will guide you to publishing sources that offer music that fits the context of this community.

Hospitality issues. One of the ways we can be hospitable to the Generation X community is to make food available during our worship services. Both Spirit Garage, Minneapolis, Minnesota, and Forest Hill Church, Charlotte, North Carolina, offer gourmet coffee and tea to worshipers to take with them to worship. These congregations do this because they have recognized that at almost any informal public gathering there is food. This is true for poetry readings in coffee houses and for rock concerts in stadiums. For Gen Xers, food is simply part of public interaction. That may mean that your congregation will need to review and revise its guidelines on food in the worship space. For Generation Xers, bringing food into the worship space is about creating a relaxing and safe atmosphere. Our Lord offered this kind of hospitality to his disciples when he broke bread with them on the night he was betrayed.

Media technology

Using media technology in worship can mean significant finances. Ultimately your congregation will need to invest both in an appropriate sound system as well as a computer and VCR-driven video system. Serving people who grew up with multi-sensate ways of learning makes it important to address the multiple ways they experience and process information. The following is a list of the basic equipment you will need to purchase for your worship leadership team:

Audio equipment:

16-channel mixer

2 to 4 amplifiers

2 main speakers and stands

2 monitor speakers

Microphones and stands for each vocalist

Video equipment:

Large projection screen

Recently manufactured computer

LCD projector

Videocassette recorder

In 1999, the cost of an inexpensive sound system ran between $4000 and $6000. The cost of an inexpensive video system was $4500 to $7000.

The use of this technology does not mean that the Generation X community wants to worship it. In fact, half-hearted technological efforts done on a congregation's limited budget may not succeed in connecting with Gen Xers, because they have grown up with and expect more sophisticated technology. The point is to get the job done as simply as possible. Regardless, the technology should remain in the background, invisible to the worshiper. Use only enough of the sound system as the musicians and preacher require. Use only the video technology you need to invite people into worship in a user-friendly way.

Starting simply

If you are in a congregation with limited resources you may wonder how you can reach this community with the resources you have. Remember that if God calls you to reach this community with the gospel, then God will also provide all the resources you need. That's why prayer is so important. It connects your vision with God's vision.

Remember also that your next important resource is people. If the congregation has, or a few key leaders have, a passion for this kind of worship, the creativity will flow. The exciting thing about indigenous worship is that solutions tend to flow more from the creativity of those involved than from any merchandise catalog. The point is not to be fancy, but to be faithful and effective.

WHAT'S AT STAKE?

Here you are, ready to consider what worship might look like in your setting. Now why would you do this? Why is it worth it? What's at stake in all this?

What's at stake is the lives of people like David Crowder, currently the worship leader at University Baptist Church, Waco, Texas. Before he became part of that community, he had little use for the church. Been there, done that. And it had almost nothing to do with the experiences of his life. But someone took the time to speak the good news of Jesus in a way that connected with him. And someone took the effort to call together a community of God's people who would reach out to people like him and speak their language. And that has made all the difference in the world. ✻

WORSHIP PLANNING HELPS

This process is best done with a worship planning team rather than with a single individual. Such a team should consist of at least:

1. The primary pastor for this service,

2. The music leader for this service,

3. Several people who represent those who will be reached by this service.

It's important that every member of the team be excited about and committed to the ministry of this particular service. Conflicting commitments and goals will stop this planning process in its tracks.

Listening to your context

I. Opportunities for conversation

Form a group that represents those God has called you to reach with your worship service and engage in honest conversation with them. Here are some questions to help you shape your conversation with them. Rather than directly asking all these questions of those who gather, use these questions to identify topics for your conversation. After the meeting, review these questions and record your responses.

What is their average age?

What is their racial/ethnic makeup?

What education level have most achieved?

What is their most preferred way of getting information?

What is their least preferred way of getting information?

What do they do for recreation (for example, concerts, sports, movies)?

What life experiences do they have in common?

What do you know about their general outlook on life?

What values do they have in common?

What life goals do they share?

What do they see as challenges to those goals?

What do you know about the music they listen to?

How does it shape their goals and values?

How do they regard the church?

How do they regard worship?

What kind of worship experience would motivate them to take a second look at the church?

2. Looking at demographics

Access at least two of the sources listed in this chapter for statistical demographics information about your community.

How does this information compare with the conversations you had with the group you gathered?

Where do the statistics and the experience of your conversation differ?

What do you think might be the reason for the differences?

3. A visit to the music store

With help from a someone in your conversation group, purchase or borrow several compact discs representative of the music listened to by participants in the conversation group. Spend some time listening to them.

What do the lyrics tell you about the hopes, fears, and values of the people who typically buy these CDs?

What does the music tell you about what you might use in your worship service?

4. Attending a concert

If you live in or near an area that offers performances by popular musicians on a regular basis, attend one that features a performer or musical style that is popular with your conversation group. This will help you experience not only what kind of music Xers listen to but how they interact in a public gathering.

What was your strongest impression of this event? What are the implications for worship planning?

In what ways does a Generation X concert have ritual structures similar to a worship service?

What might you adopt from this concert into your worship services?

Basic worship priorities

The following questions will help you center your team around a common biblical vision for your worship service.

From the Scriptures, what do you as a team believe God desires for people to experience in worship?

How is this reflected in your denominational tradition?

List the things that could hinder what God desires for worshipers.

What might you do to remove these barriers?

What are your denomination's "bottom lines" in terms of flexibility in worship?

Worship service planning

Here are some key areas to consider as you plan your worship services week to week. Remember to keep in mind God's desire for the worshiper as well as your context.

Theme

What is the primary message you wish to communicate through this week's worship service?

Environment

What elements of environment (for example, art, banners, plants, incense) will you employ to strengthen the worship experience in your physical space?

Worship pattern

Consider the following ritual elements:

Gathering

Hearing the Word

Feasting at the Lord's Supper

Sending into witness and service

With these and other components, how might your planning team structure the worship service so that it supports the communication of God's word to the worshiper?

Use of media

What media resources (video, computers, LCD projectors, sound systems) do you have at hand?

How could they be appropriately incorporated into worship?

Worship music

Regardless of style and context, here are some general criteria to observe when choosing music for worship.

Regarding the music itself:

Is it interesting and engaging to those you are serving?

Does the music fit the text?

Is it easy to sing for guests?

Is it memorable?

Is it durable?

Regarding the lyrics:

Do the lyrics reflect the truth of Scripture in terms of God's commands, promises, and self-disclosure?

Do the lyrics reflect the truth of who we are as sinful yet priceless people before God?

Do the lyrics connect contextually the with those God has called you to serve (in other words, brokenness, abandonment, true friendship, hope)?

When using secular music, do the lyrics connect tightly enough with the message so that you don't have to spend a lot of time explaining why you used this song?

Based on what you have learned about this generation's music in particular, what styles make sense for this worship service?

Within these styles, what selections would work best to support the theme of this service?

Where in the worship service should they be placed?

Here are some possible categories for music placement:

• Music of praise

• Music of confession

• Music that connects to the message (sacred and secular)

• Music that proclaims God's promises

• Music for Holy Communion

• Music of renewal and commitment

Use of drama, dance, video

How might the use of dance, drama, video clips, and so forth support the theme of this worship service?

What resources exist in your community to make these possible?

Preaching style

What shape will preaching take in this service?

Visit any congregations in your area that are ministering effectively to this generation. What did you learn from them about preaching style?

Worship evaluation

Constant evaluation will help the worship planning team learn whether the worshiper experiences what you believe God intends. For these questions you will need an evaluation team that asks the following questions of people as they leave the worship service. Be sure that your team thanks everyone they survey.

1. What impressed you most about the worship service?

2. What did you find to be most helpful?

3. In the sermon, what did you find helpful or meaningful?

4. What are your impressions of the music?

5. Overall, is there anything in the worship service that you would have added, changed, or omitted?

Keep in mind that the information you need will not arise out of a single service; rather it will reveal itself through trends. That means you will need to ask these questions over a four- to six-week period.

making *disciples*

Mark A. Peterson

Mark lives with his family in Boise, Idaho, where he has served as pastor of Community Lutheran Church since its beginning in 1996.

With the enthusiasm of a knight charged with a special task, I set out from my home into the warmth of Boise's mid-afternoon March air to knock on doors in my new community. My knees were weak, my palms sweaty, my nerves shaken as I timidly knocked on the first door that spring day in 1996. Questions plagued my mind. Who would answer? Would they be angry at me? Would they slam the door in my face? Or, would they be an honest inquirer and become the first members of a church that did not yet exist?

And, how had I landed in this place?

AN UNFAMILIAR PLACE

On the first day of 1996, late at night, my family and I had arrived in the dark, cold, and lonely town of Boise, Idaho. We had moved fifteen hundred miles away from familiar places, familiar friends, familiar ministry, to this most completely unfamiliar place.

When we landed at the airport, no one was there to meet us. Standing in our driveway as the taxi pulled away, neither a welcome committee nor a jolly church council member greeted us with an open and outstretched hand. We were completely alone. It was the loneliest time of our lives.

We were not to remain alone long, however. My job was to build a new church, though I had no idea how to go about this process. I had no experience in such things. But, I did know, beyond a shadow of a doubt, that I had been called here, to this place, to gather a group of people and speak the gospel message to them, opening the way for them to become disciples of Jesus Christ. The question that presented itself, however, was "How am I going to gather this group of people together?" I knew absolutely no one.

It seemed natural that gathering a group of people together should begin with community door-knocking. This meant going from door to door in a systematic, laid-out manner, to become more acquainted with the community and invite people to join the fellowship.

This was a daunting task. Surrounding me were more than two thousand homes, and in each of these homes lived people——families, parents, grandparents, children, single adults, teenagers—the future congregation of Community of Life Church. But, I did not know them and they did not know me. And, as I was to find out, they knew very little of the Jesus Christ that I knew, and even less of what it means to be his follower.

So there I was, standing on that first stoop, a closed door in front of my face, with questions racing through my mind, until I realized that forty-five seconds had passed. Suddenly a new question presented itself, "Is there anyone home?"

To my relief, no one was home! After leaving a brochure, I moved on. I continued knocking on one door after the next, and my fear of being scorned by hostile homeowners passed with every conversation.

A week before Easter, after a month or more of many conversations, invitations tendered, and brochures left on doors, I received a voice mail message: "Hi, my name is Donna. I came home from work today and found the brochure for your church on my kitchen counter. I picked it up and read through it. It occurred to me that this is exactly what I am looking for. I don't quite know how to explain what I am feeling, or why I am feeling this way, but I think I really need to talk to you."

I quickly returned Donna's telephone call. By the conclusion of our conversation, we had set up a meeting for the following evening. I was excited, nervous, and apprehensive about the meeting, and as I found out later, Donna was too.

The conversation that took place at Donna's home that evening has forever changed my ministry. The way I look at the world, the way I am a pastor, the whole focus of the newly developing church has changed.

AN UNFAMILIAR GOD

Donna was and is a remarkable person in many ways—her candor regarding questions of faith, her willingness to learn, her naiveté regarding things that I had forever taken for granted, and her complete lack of knowledge concerning the Bible.

The conversation at her home that evening began with Donna telling me a bit about her life. She grew up in a divorced home and was left to fend for herself for as long as she could remember. She left home at age sixteen and lived in various places. Later she had a child with her boyfriend; they had a troubled relationship and they finally separated. She was alone again, but now accompanied by her only child. She raised her son the best she could, giving him everything and all that she had to offer, until one day he asked her a question that she couldn't answer. "Mom," he asked, "what is Easter all about?"

As I sat with her that evening she recounted this story and then asked me the same question, "What is Easter all about?" I had never been asked such a question before and didn't quite know how to respond to her. I had always taken for granted that people knew the purpose and meaning of Easter. Never before had I encountered such a question. So I set out on a journey that continues to this day.

As we sat in her living room that evening, Donna was told of Easter and its meaning for the first time ever. In terms that made complete sense to me, I explained how Jesus was brought to trial, how he was convicted and killed. In the best way I could I told her of the wonder of Jesus being raised three days following his death. It made complete sense to me. But she looked at me with bewilderment and asked, "But who is Jesus?"

I sat in stunned silence. Questions once again raced through my mind. In disbelief I silently asked myself, "Is she serious? Does she really not know who Jesus is? How can this be?" I sat unable to answer her because, for the second time that evening, I was confronted with yet another new question——how to explain who Jesus is to someone who has never heard.

Again, I did the best I could in my attempt to explain to her the person and story of Jesus Christ. I fumbled. I grasped at concepts and theology that I had been taught in seminary. I went into lengthy detail retelling some of the stories that are contained in the Bible about what Jesus did and how he lived his life. When I began to talk about the Bible, I noticed the same bewildered face. She asked plainly, "But, what is that Bible?"

For the third time in less than one hour I was confronted with yet another question that I was unprepared to answer, and no doubt she saw similar bewilderment in my face as I struggled with the answer to her question.

One more time, I did my best to explain to her what the Bible is and why it is important to Christians. I briefly outlined what is contained in the Bible and mentioned some of the stories and songs and poems that are in it. I mentioned Moses and Abraham. Then, for the fourth time that evening, bewilderment covered her face: "Who are Moses and Abraham?"

THE FIRST GENERATION BORN WITHOUT GOD

This story of Donna is not atypical. We live in a world full of people like her, and their numbers are increasing. There is an emerging generation of people with the same questions, people with the same naiveté, people with the same ignorance concerning matters of the Christian faith.

These people are my contemporaries and we are known by many different labels. Generation X is one of them. Regardless of what this generation is called, there is a common current that seems to run through this generation—they know very little of the Jesus that the Christian church proclaims; and even less about the Bible. Additionally, this generation is not familiar with the traditional Christian church that many of us know and are comfortable with. To them it may seem as a dark, cold, lonely, and completely unfamiliar place.

On the other hand, we find these people to be very interested in spiritual matters. There is a rich desire to test spiritual disciplines, which may be why Donna contacted me initially. Donna, and those of her generation, may not be familiar with the Christian tradition, but they are spiritual in nature.

OUR CALLING AND THE CHALLENGE

We have experienced a massive shift in our society that has occurred over the past twenty years, from a "churched" culture to an "unchurched" culture. The sad thing is that, by and large, the church has functioned as if this was not the case. We have continued to function as if this shift has not occurred. We have gotten stuck in a paradigm that does not work with Generation X.

The question that presents itself, then, is what are we going to do about this? What about those people like Donna? What about this generation of seeking and searching men and women? How will they know? How can we engage them? How can we reach these people so that the Holy Spirit can grow them into faithful followers of Jesus Christ? How do we make disciples of those who know very little of Jesus Christ and of the message contained in the Bible?

These questions go to the core issue of what it means to be a church in mission in the twenty-first century. And what makes this task even more difficult is determining how to tell people about Jesus Christ when most preconceptions they have of organized Christian religion are negative. This is particularly true for those we call postmoderns, or Generation X.

The period in which we live has been described as more similar to first century Christianity than any other century. There are many reasons for this. First of all, Generation X doesn't know the Christian story. Second, the generation we seek to engage is often skeptical and at times hostile toward those who claim to be Christian. We have a difficult job—not only presenting the gospel but making disciples of people who don't know about Jesus and may even be hostile towards him.

No matter how difficult and large the challenge may be, it is our calling to reach all people with the gospel. It is our calling to make disciples of all people. But how do we do that for the postmodern generation?

DISCIPLING A GENERATION

The definition of discipleship has changed over many years. For Boomers and their parents, discipleship could be described as the process of becoming indoctrinated into a specific set of beliefs. For faith traditions that baptize infants, it meant baptism started the discipleship process and continued with years of Sunday school, Christmas programs, and vacation Bible school. Eventually—finally—the young person confirmed his or her faith in a graduation-like ceremony. For other faith traditions, baptism followed years of instruction during childhood, but the results are similar. Once a young person was baptized or confirmed, then one had "graduated" and was seen as a full-fledged member of the church. Often the learning and discipling process ended at this point, as expectations of the member shifted from learning Bible stories and church doctrine to contributing time and money.

The life experience of Generation X can help the church see discipleship in a different way. Discipleship is a lifelong growing and deepening in faith that has no ending. Discipleship is a process of becoming a committed follower of Jesus Christ that can last a lifetime—not graduating into full membership in a congregation or becoming a Lutheran or Methodist or Baptist. For instance, most of the people involved in Community of Life Church are participating not because it is a Lutheran church, but because we speak the message of Jesus Christ. They have found hope, life, meaning, and purpose for their lives, not a particular set of denominational beliefs. Thus, the process of discipleship may not mean becoming a "member" of anything other than the body of Christ.

This may be seen as quite a radical concept by older generations who built our churches and cathedrals and whose expectation is that Generation X will commit to the same institution. But, of course, it is not radical at all. It is getting back to the real focus of what Jesus meant when he told his followers to "go and make disciples"(Matthew 28:19). For our grandparents though, it's a matter of survival. "Who will inhabit this facility after we are gone?" they ask. Generation X says, "Who cares?"

For Generation X, the principle at work is not the building or institution, but a life changed and a relationship engaged. It is about transformation. It is faithfully following in the footsteps of the One who has gone before us. First must come commitment to Christ, then commitment to the church and its larger cause will naturally follow.

In the discipleship process of Generation X, one of the things that we must allow for is a significant period of time for people to test the waters. Often they will become actively involved in the congregation, attend Bible studies, play in a worship band, serve on teams, and so forth, while never actually becoming a full-fledged member of the church. Many engage in a spiritual journey with their participation in the church, but have no desire for membership. They may seem from the outside to have all the hallmarks of a "member," but actually their participation is part of the exploration process. It is their way to engage Christ and attempt to be faithful to him.

One of the things that must be considered in regard to this is communion practice. For earlier generations, "truth" is what someone in authority tells them is the "truth." Many people may still have a vague image of Walter Cronkite signing off his newscast each evening with the final, and very certain, words, "And that's the way it is." There was no room for debate, no room for another point of view.

For Generation X, however, unlike generations that have proceeded them, experience is truth, not what someone else tells them. Having experienced something, they then can make a judgment whether it holds authority for them. Knowing this, a congregation seeking to reach Generation X will have to struggle with the question of whether or not people ought to be receiving communion before they are baptized. If they are allowed to experience communion and the presence of Jesus Christ through their participation with the rest of the body of Christ, they may then find the truth in the sacrament. For Generation X, first comes the experience and then truth, not the other way around.

The main point here is this: As long as we the church continue to insist that Generation X commit to the church before committing to Christ we will be fighting a losing battle. Many Xers see people doggedly committed to an organization—people who attend worship and frequent church activities, but whose daily lives seem unaffected by their relationship with Christ. What is primary for Generation X is the relationship with Christ—not membership in the church. We must allow them to experiment, experience, test, ask questions, engage in a relationship, and continue along a journey toward Christ that may take many months or even years.

Discipleship, for all of us, is discovering who Jesus Christ is and engaging in a faithful journey of following him. It's not a set of doctrines or beliefs that are held by all; it's not becoming a member of a congregation; it's not paying for a building campaign. Rather, it is a gradual exploration and participation with the faith community into discovery of Jesus Christ. It is a journey that no one ever graduates from, a journey that continues for a lifetime.

RELATIONSHIPS ENGAGED, LIVES CHANGED

Discipleship and evangelism often happen simultaneously for Generation X. If the question for evangelism is "How can we share the good news of Jesus Christ in a way that people can hear it?" Then, the question for discipleship is "How can we make their entrance or return to the faith community a positive one, one that will set their feet on a journey to a greater and more meaningful life of faith?" A conversation at a coffee shop with an unchurched Generation X friend can be as much discipleship as it is evangelism. Discipleship begins the moment a person encounters the faith community. As a Christian community we must strive to make that entrance into the body an easy transition.

The challenge with discipling this generation is that there aren't ten steps to follow in a discipleship process; it's simply not a linear process. But there are some common principles and effective approaches.

- Discipleship begins with relationship. We must engage Generation X with open arms and listen to pains and hurts.

- We address their questions, many of which are basic questions of faith, life's meaning, their purpose.

- We create points of entry into the faith community that take into account their life situations, questions, unfamiliarity with the Christian faith, and desire for authentic community.

- We place priority on community, authentic community, and

experience of the Holy.

- We help them discern their spiritual gifts as they live them out in the faith community and world.

- We as leaders establish coaching and mentoring relationships to teach the faith and develop leaders.

- We address traditions, governance structures, and definitions of membership that need to change for us to effectively reach people with the gospel.

Relationships characterized by listening

To disciple Generation X we must relate to them in a way that is sincere, authentic, loving, accepting, welcoming, and most impor-tant—free of judgment. The stereotypes this generation has regarding the church are often very difficult to overcome. One of the most effective ways to begin the discipleship process and over-come these stereotypes is to engage in a caring relationship with them. This can happen anywhere, at any time, at any place. Usually the relationship is conceived outside the confines of the church, such as a gathering at someone's home or with a group of friends at a coffee shop, or perhaps at a child's soccer game.

Within the safety of an authentic relationship, we then can stand beside them and embody the Spirit of Christ to them. Over a period of time, questions can be asked and answered in a nonthreatening environment and barriers can be overcome. It is through our listening that we can know that their story is in fact our story. It is only through this type of loving by engaging that we will begin to grasp for ourselves the depth of the spiritual pain that is being expressed. And it is only then that we can begin to hear the questions that people are asking. It is difficult for some-one who is not of this generation to know what the questions are. Therefore, listening is the beginning point of the relationship.

Listening is exactly what took place as Community of Life Church began in 1996. The entire church gathered together—all fifteen people—and spoke of what they hoped their new church would become. Dreams were shared. Visions were explored. Hopes were expressed. Questions were asked.

When St. Andrew Lutheran Church, Waukesha, Wisconsin, decided to reach out to young adults in its community, they too began with a process of listening. The pastor gathered ten people from eighteen to thirty years old for meetings on a monthly basis to discuss and dream about what a new worship service might look like in order to reach Gen Xers. The question that Pastor Larry Harpster posed to this group was, "What would it look like if you could throw out all the rules and create something that you would come to?" As a result of the listening, a new worship service was planned. It was held on Sunday evening and had the feel of a rock concert with faith witnessing midway through the service. The sermon was presented in a dialogue format and the congregation was asked to break up into small groups to discuss the topic with one another.

Key to starting a ministry to reach Generation X is gathering a group of us together and listening to the voices that emerge. Discipling Generation X begins with caring relationships characterized by listening to our dreams and hearing our questions.

Addressing the primary questions

Through the process of listening we can begin to hear that this generation is asking a unique set of questions. Typically the questions are ones of life's meaning and an individual's purpose in it. They also may be unaware of the stories contained in the Bible. When they encounter the Christian church, they often have basic questions such as: Who is Jesus? What is the Bible? What makes your God so special? These are primary questions. These are the questions that Donna asked me.

In responding to these questions, what is suggested is that we give people an "unplugged" version of the gospel story. We do this by smartening up our practice of teaching the faith, not dumbing it down. We give this generation the raw material of the gospel—the basic stories of life and death—the primary issues of faith.

Perhaps the best sermon one can give on Sunday morning is simply to stand up and retell a story that has been told for thousands of years. "There is this cool story," we can say, "of when Jesus heals a blind man with spit and dirt." From that moment on they are captivated. Why? Because basic questions are being addressed: "What was Jesus' purpose?" "How did he interact with other people?" "Why did he die?"

Small-group Bible studies also are great places to gather people and invite them to ask their questions in an environment that is nonthreatening and caring. The principle behind small-group ministry is that it is a place where people can come together and form caring relationships and, in the process, grow in a life of faith and have the freedom to ask the very basic questions they may struggle with. Care must be taken as you begin small-group ministry to inform people that those with questions, or people who are seeking and searching, or those who don't "have it all together" are welcomed and encouraged to attend.

Joyful Spirit Lutheran Church in Bolingbrook, Illinois, experienced rapid growth as a result of small-group ministry in the initial years of its development. Andy Hagen, the pastor of the church, mentions that people like to gather not only to get to know one another but to discuss basic issues of faith development in a small group of caring people. "So much of the church and faith was new to them, and we found small groups a perfect way for people to ask basic questions of faith," Hagen said.

Mentoring relationships are perhaps the best and most effective way for people to have their primary questions asked and answered. In and through the context of a one-to-one relationship people can grow into a life of faith by watching, inquiring, and practicing. Often this kind of mentoring can be done within the context of a small group.

Lecture-style Bible studies are another way to address primary questions. There are many introductory Bible survey classes with supporting curricula that can be offered to lay the groundwork of the Christian story.

Recognizing points of entry

Another aspect of the discipleship process is creating points of entry into the faith community. The point of entry for each Gen Xer is unique. There are as many ways to engage people of this generation in a journey of discipleship as there are people.

For the generations that preceded us, it seemed a bit more cut-and-dried. For the GI (born 1909–1933) and Builder (born 1933–45) generations, the connecting point with the church is working toward a common cause or meeting a common need, which a large organization is better positioned to accomplish. Thus denominational structure and hierarchy are accepted by this generation as necessary and useful. Such institutions and their leaders are, generally, a trusted authority.

For Boomers the point of entry to congregations and the church is meeting an individual's "felt need." The life question Boomers are asking is "How do I make my life work?" So to engage this group of people, congregations need to ask, "What need are these people expressing, can the church meet that need, and if so, how?" Commonly, the felt needs for the Boomer generation have been marital problems, issues with raising children, financial concerns, and so forth.

Some churches offer small groups on "How to raise a toddler" or "Dealing with divorce" to create side-door points of entry. Many congregations have found that addressing these felt needs has proven to be successful in reaching the Boomer generation. But this approach does not work for Generation X.

What is the point of entry for Generation X? In *Jesus for a New Generation*, Kevin Graham Ford writes, "Maybe as you read about the challenges of communicating the story of Jesus with this generation, you have begun to conclude, It's hopeless! Thirteeners are a closed, unreachable generation! Nothing could be further from the truth. Thirteeners are very open to the Christian story right now—if it is presented in an effective and appropriate way. They may be closed to old, outmoded evangelistic methods, but not to the story itself. The Bible speaks directly to the pain of Generation X, and its message is targeted on Xer yearnings and needs—the need for hope, the need for meaning, the need for community, the need for empowerment and a sense of direction in life" (*Jesus for a New Generation*, Kevin Graham Ford, Jim Denney, George Gallup Jr. [Intro]. Downer's Grove, Ill.: InterVarsity, 1995, p. 173).

Generation X wants the real stuff. Generation X wants the raw material of the Bible, and they want it presented to them in a raw, authentic way. The message of God's love, which is revealed through biblical accounts, can address their spiritual experiences—hopelessness, fear, discouragement, pain, loss, the need for direction.

One must keep this in mind when preaching. At Community of Life I stand up on Sunday morning with no pulpit and no written script. I preach in plain, ordinary, conversational English about the life and death struggles contained in the Bible. In a narrative format, I speak to the people about their pain and loss—about their joy and celebration. It's not slick, it's not polished, it's not prepackaged. Listeners get the feeling it is very real and spoken from personal experience.

The various points of entry for this generation, then, must have in common a real and meaningful encounter with the Holy— with Christ himself, with the Word. No tricks. No gimmicks. No three or five or ten steps to happiness, success, perfect kids, or anything else. For them, life just is not that simple, and if you try to involve them in such an approach, they will run the other way, which is what has been happening to congregations all across the country.

At Community of Life we began our small-group ministry program with great fanfare by offering several studies developed by a well-known and reputable Christian publisher. We utterly failed in our efforts to get groups organized and running. It was very discouraging. What we found is that people were more interested in in-depth Bible studies. They wanted an approach in which they could open the Bible, study it, and use it. Even those people brand new to the Christian faith found these types of studies much more fulfilling and meaningful in their daily lives. It was in and through these studies that their questions of faith could be asked, where they encountered the Word, and their lives began to change.

Mars Hill Fellowship in Seattle recognizes the importance of a meaningful encounter with the Holy and how this encounter changes lives. During the summer months they schedule outdoor services where people are encouraged to invite their friends. At these services time is given for individuals to stand up and give a testimony of how God has worked in their lives and how their lives have been changed as a result. Often their friends and relatives will respond, "You know, I just knew that you had changed recently, and now I know why!"

Creating authentic community

Those churches that have become successful at reaching Generation X have found one thing common to this generation— they recognize that Generation X is in search of relationship. They do not want doctrine; they are not looking for practical steps for making their lives work. Generation X wants to be loved. Generation X wants to engage in a meaningful faith journey within the context of a relationship.

A recent article in *Changing Church Perspectives* says this: "Community is central to the twenty-first century church. Today, we are a culture of fractured families and changing social structures. We are time-starved and isolated by distance, work, individualistic pursuits, and even our neighborhoods. Yet, we are created for community. Community in the church of the future is more than just making relationships or being in a small group. It is an expression of the gospel. It is both hermeneutic and apologetic.

The church has nothing to show other than the exhibit of how we live in community with Christ at the center. Community is not an extra or bonus. It is the essence of what Christians have to offer" ("Church, the New Edge," from *Changing Church Perspectives*, April-June 1999. Copyright © Leadership Network. Used by permission).

Community is the essence of being together as the body of Christ—in worship, in fellowship, in prayer and study. Community is more than just hanging out, it is experiencing and living in the presence of Christ.

Mars Hill Fellowship has asked people to gather in homes during a four-week period with six or eight other people with the simple purpose of sharing a meal together. From these meals community is created and relationships are born.

There is no gimmick here. Over and over again, those churches that are successful at discipling Generation X have found ways to build community and the relationships that are fostered through this community. Specifically this may be a small-group Bible study that meets together regularly for prayer, study of Scripture, and simple fellowship.

Contained in Donna's story at the beginning of this chapter, is her deep-seated need for community. From a very early age she was alone. She had no one to turn to. She left her home when she was a teenager and was forced to fend for herself. Early on in her relationship with a congregation, she became involved in a small-group Bible study. The group met regularly, once a week or more. It was in and through her participation with this group of people that she embarked on a journey of faith that continues to unfold for her even to this day.

Some churches have found that recovery groups dealing with issues such as alcohol and chemical abuse are effective ways for engaging this generation in a meaningful faith journey.

Other churches have found that social advocacy groups that gather for the specific purpose of meeting a community need have opened hearts to the presence of Jesus Christ. For instance, Spirit Garage, a Lutheran congregation in Minneapolis, brings groups of people together numerous times throughout the year for specific outreach activities that allow people to give of themselves in creative and meaningful ways. Pastor Pam Fickenscher said, "Allowing people to give of themselves without any expectation of return is a powerful and needed thing in one's spiritual journey." Most of these social advocacy groups, she says, allow people to build relationships in a nonthreatening, time-limited environment.

Other churches have found that seeker or inquirer classes have been successful. These classes are designed simply to get people together to form community, while in the process, answering questions and engaging in faith discovery. The key, again, to any of these groups is an authentic community that gathers for care, relationship, and spiritual development in a nonthreatening atmosphere.

The Internet. One unique and booming strategy that is working in many congregations nationwide for forming community and relationships is the World Wide Web. This generation feels more at home on the Internet than they do in church, so it is only natural for congregations to begin to use the Internet as a discipleship tool. Congregations recognizing this as a ministry opportunity have developed home pages with specific times people can gather in a "virtual community" for discussion and fellowship. Other churches have set up meetings in which participants discuss any number of questions. The intriguing thing about the Internet and the "virtual community" it creates is that all of this takes place from within the comfort and familiarity of one's own home. You barely even have to lift a finger, so to speak, to engage in dialogue with people. Relationship is created, dialogue is engaged, and the process of discipleship can begin. In the future more ministry will take place through the Internet than over the television—and perhaps than in our churches.

At Community of Life we have set up an Internet list-serve meeting where individuals from home can engage in a cyberspace meeting with other people in the congregation. We have discussed many and various topics ranging from baptism to communion to world politics. This has become an effective way for us to reach into the homes of many individuals who have never yet participated in a worship service at Community of Life, but yet remain engaged with us in our ministry.

Another church, Joy Lutheran Church, in Gurnee, Illinois, uses the Internet to send daily devotionals to people who subscribe to the list. The devotional is written by three or four people within the church and compiled by an editor. Currently there are 220 subscribers to the list, which is growing by four or five people per day. Many of the people on the list have never attended Joy, but have a daily contact with a spiritual community as a result of the list.

Discerning spiritual gifts

As people are part of a Christian community, as they encounter the holy and explore faith questions, they grow in their relationship to God and to others. Part of their exploration and growth includes discerning spiritual gifts. Identifying spiritual gifts has worked well with Generation X as long as such a program combines the discernment with a process of spiritual growth. There is a plethora of spiritual gift inventories available on the market today, designed to assist churches in identifying the particular spiritual gifts of individuals within the congregation. With Generation X, these inventories ought to be used in a manner that would coordinate with a small-group ministry so that people discover their spiritual gifts as they are at the same time engaged with others in building community and learning about the Christian faith. As their spiritual gifts are identified, leaders can identify places where they can use their gifts. A ministry team governance structure (see below) is a helpful framework for shepherding them in developing their gifts.

A ministry that has taken a unique approach to spiritual gifts analysis is University Baptist Church in Waco, Texas. Pastor Kyle Lake described that people are encouraged to attend a "UBC 101" class where individuals are asked to fill out a gift inventory that can be found on the Internet. The inventory is made up of seventy-five questions. Once people fill it out, it is scored immediately. People are then plugged into groups and teams and given an opportunity to experience "hands on" ministry in their particular areas of giftedness.

Mentoring leaders

The pastor plays an important role in the discipleship process and functions like a coach or a spiritual mentor. The pastor spends much of his or her time building relationships and "coaching" people as they explore the faith and identify and develop their area of giftedness. To be clear, coaching is different than teaching or telling. Coaching is standing beside and walking with people, and leading them to greater awareness and capability—not above or before them but along with and beside them.

Not only the pastor can serve a mentor. Within a ministry team structure, the leader of the team often has at least one "apprentice" who may function as an understudy. The mentoring and coaching process then is multiplied as the apprentice assumes a position of leadership. The process then repeats itself from one leader to the next.

In this approach people are grown into positions of leadership, not thrown into them. They are not elected into official offices and given immediate authority over ministry issues. Rather, people slowly assume more responsibility and develop more competence in an area of ministry.

Redefining the structure

To effectively reach people with the gospel, we must also examine long-standing practices and governance structures that no longer serve a useful purpose or, in some cases, create barriers to including and involving new people.

Many churches throughout the country have found the process of moving Generation X into church leadership to be a challenge. Why is this? One reason is that the governing structure of most churches does not fit with how Generation X views the world. Most structures of governing in churches today are based on a top-down management style—the pyramid structure. At the top of the pyramid is the pastor and the church council, through which decisions in matters of ministry and method must pass—the budget, worship practices, the color of carpet in the sanctuary—often these decisions need final ratification by this highest level of governance.

A pyramid style of governing—the one used by most churches today—has little or no value to a Generation Xer. Why? Because such a pyramid structure offers people authority based solely upon the position they hold or the title they have. But Generation X is the first generation born that has access to knowledge without having first to go through an authority figure. It is well-documented, probably not least of which from your own experience, that Generation X has little regard for authority based on hierarchy. They simply have no use for it. What matters to them and what becomes authority to them is their personal experience. They have been told over and over again by people in authority how they should act, what they should believe, where they should go, what they can and cannot do, and so forth. It's like a broken record, and such people hold little to no authority over them. But, if they have experienced it for themselves, if they have lived and breathed and felt and smelled it from their own personal experience, that is what holds authority for them. Perhaps this is where Nike sportswear company gets its slogan, "Just do it."

For Xers a pastor gains his or her authority not because of the office that is held, but through the example of an authentic life lived as a disciple of Jesus Christ. A pastor's authority results from the experience that people have over time with that pastor.

In more and more congregations, there is a new paradigm of church governance at work. It is comprised of two basic principles: (1) it is participatory (team structured), and (2) egalitarian or nonauthoritarian (permission giving). In short it is a paradigm that is relationally based and empowering.

Ministry teams. It is through a relationally based and Christ-centered approach that a system of governing and leadership development for Generation X should begin.

Community of Life Church began in 1997 with a group of six people sitting together in a living room studying the Bible. It became quickly apparent that the process of developing these people into disciples of Jesus Christ was of primary importance. The group gathered together, they studied together, they prayed for one another. Relationships grew with one another and Jesus Christ was certainly present.

Over the course of time, this group grew in its commitment to Jesus Christ and it grew larger. The problem that began to present itself was "How do we govern and lead this group of people who have gathered?"

For a long period, the church leadership consisted of a small group of committed members called "The Vision Team." This team served as the body that governed the church. They managed the daily nuts and bolts and the administration of the congregation. They gave it direction, they evaluated its past, they dreamed about its future, and they served as a support for the pastor.

The pastor formed the Vision Team, the governing body of the church, first as a small group of people who gathered for study, fellowship, prayer, and spiritual growth. They experienced the presence of the Holy in a relationally based, small group. It was in and through this process that the Vision Team began to assume leadership responsibilities. Notice that first in the process of leadership development was a strong, faithful commitment to and center in Jesus Christ, and second were relationships built with others on the team.

The Vision Team also functioned as a team. It was not a committee that had a chairperson who held all the authority, but it was an empowered team in which all people held equal authority, including the pastor. The same can be said for the Mission Board structure that now directs the long-term ministry of the congregation.

Those churches across the United States that are successful in reaching Generation X rely heavily on the team structure of ministry. They are remarkably relational in nature. Also, no one group, or one person, or one area of ministry, stands in authority over any other. All have equal value and power and are equal in the decision-making process.

Permission-giving ministry. The second principle of this new paradigm of church governance is that it is remarkably permission-giving. There is no large structure or leadership pyramid that people have to work through in order to make specific ministry decisions. Many of the decisions regarding ministry choices come directly from the "grassroots" or from the team structure that infuses the congregation.

King of Kings Lutheran Church in Shelby Township, Michigan, reorganized its governance around central issues contained within its mission statement. After a period of developing a mission statement, the leadership of the congregation communicated it to the people in a variety of forms—bulletins, sermons, banners, newsletters, and so forth. The congregation then restructured its governance around the new mission statement that pushed them into a mission-oriented and permission-giving ministry. Ministry teams began to undertake the bulk of the ministry being done at the church. The turning point for the congregation was understanding who was in control with this new leadership system—was it the council, the pastor, or the loudest complainer? According to Pastor Louis Forney, "We became convinced that if we understood the Holy Spirit to be present in the life of God's people, we needed to trust those people." The next step was obvious to them, "After articulating our mission and restructuring for ministry, we took the next step. Since God is in charge, we decided to let people carry out the work God has given to us. The mission of the congregation became the direction of our ministry. We stopped discussing everything everywhere, and just did ministry. Since that time, self-starting and self-directing ministry teams have grown up everywhere. They are encouraged to see and meet needs. If something is consistent with our mission, it happens. No one stops ministry from moving forward! Responsibility for ministry rests in the hands of the people of God—where it belongs. In some ways, the church has turned upside-down. Leaders teach people the mission and equip them to do ministry. We give people what they need to do what they are here to do" ("The Discipling Congregation," Division for Congregational Ministries, Summer 1998. Copyright © 1998 the Reverend Dr. Louis R. Forney. Used by permission).

This approach to church governance looks and functions much like a multicellular organism: it lives and breathes and stretches and grows and eventually dies when its usefulness is complete. It is not hierarchical or rigidly structured in a way that stifles growth or continues on just because it has always existed. As leaders are reproduced and ministry opportunities arise, the organism grows, parts of it die, and others multiply and divide, sometimes in miraculous ways.

The evolving process of governance at Community of Life illustrates how death occurs where necessary, so that new life can emerge. After a time, the Vision Team began to lose its sense of purpose. The group felt that more "tangible" ministry issues needed to be addressed. This group evolved into a system of team leaders that were each responsible for specific areas of ministry within the fellowship. As time wore on, guidance was lacking and long-term direction was needed, so this group evolved once again into a Mission Board. The Mission Board, consisting of five team leaders and four elders, continues to function as the leadership system that steers and directs the long-range ministry of Community of Life Church. It is not without its hitches and glitches and bumps in the road, but this is the case in any organization.

THE CHALLENGE AND OUR CALL

The church's call to make disciples of Generation X is at the same time challenging and exciting. Like the early church, we are called to create relationships and communities centered in Christ and characterized by love. In these relationships, all of us discover what it means to be disciples of Jesus in the world.

Generation X by nature is the most entrepreneurial generation ever to have been born in the history of the United States and Canada. For the church to allow this entrepreneurial spirit to work will mean that things will be done differently; such change is almost always unsettling and often scary. But, change is also exactly what needs to happen for the church to reach this generation of adults and the generations that follow. We can be open to the new, varied, and creative ways God will work through each generation because God has secured the future. ✠

appendix

resources and *networks*

CONGREGATIONS

Acton-Boxborough Congregational Church
12 Concord Road
Acton, MA 01720
Phone: (978) 263-2728
Fax: (978) 264-9457
Gail Miller, pastor
Visit their Web site at: www.ultranet.com/~actoncon.org

All Saints Episcopal Church
3560 Kings River Road
Pawleys Island, SC 29585
Phone: (843) 237-4223
Fax: (843) 237-1958
Contemporary worship staff: Tim Surratt
E-mail: Timrat@allsaintspawleys.org
Visit their Web site at: www.allsaintspawleys.org

Calvary Church Newport Mesa
190 East 23rd Street
Costa Mesa, CA 92627
(714) 645-5050
Tim Celek, pastor:
E-mail: Tcelek@aol.com

Cities Vineyard Fellowship and Music
1406 West Lake Street, Suite 208
Minneapolis, MN 55408

(612) 825-2512
E-mail: info@citiesvineyard.com
Visit their Web site at: www.citiesvineyard.com

Community of Life Lutheran Church
5453 Firethorn Place
Boise, Idaho 83705
Phone: (208) 385-7020
Fax: (208) 385-0954
Mark A. Peterson, pastor
E-mail: life@micron.net
Visit their Web site at: http://netnow.micron.net/~life/

First Covenant Church of Sacramento
9000 La Rivera Drive
Sacramento, CA 95826
Phone: (916) 363-9446
Ted Smith, pastor
E-mail: For1stCov@aol.com
Visit their Web site at: http://churches.net/free/fccs.htm

Ginghamsburg UMC
6759 South County Road 25A
Tipp City, Ohio 45371
Phone: (937) 667-1069
Fax: (937) 667-5667
Michael Slaughter, pastor:
E-mail: staff@gum-net.org
Visit their Web site at: www.ginghamsburg.org

Mars Hill Fellowship
4505 University Way NE Suite 314
Seattle, WA 98105
Phone: (206) 523-3104

Mark Driscoll, pastor
E-mail: Life@marshillchurch.org
Brad Currah, music pastor
E-mail: brad@marshillchurch.org
Visit their Web site at: www.marshillchurch.org

New Hope Christian Fellowship
P.O. Box 11132
Honolulu, HI 96828
(808) 833-7717
Wayne Cordeiro, pastor

New Song Community Church
13873 National Road SW
Reynoldsburg, OH 43068
Phone: (740) 927-5015
Fax: (740) 964-0741
Chuck Long, pastor
E-mail: youmatter2@aol.com
Visit their Web site: www.youmatter.com

Park St. Church
1 Park Street
Boston, MA 02108
Phone: (617) 523-3383
Fax: (617) 523-3383
Chris Sherwood, assistant minister
E-mail: Csherwood@parkstreet.org
Visit their Web site at: www.parkstreet.org
Sunday Radio Broadcast: 11am and 6:30 P.M. WEZE (590)
Boston and WPZE (1260) and 7:30 A.M. WHOM-FM
(94.9) Mt. Washington, NH

Pathways Church
3190 South Grant Street
Englewood, CO 80110
Phone: (303) 761-9464
Fax: (303) 761-4416
Ron Johnson, pastor:
E-mail: info@pathwayschurch.org
Visit their Web site at: www.pathwayschurch.org

Spirit Garage
c/o Bethlehem Lutheran Church
4100 Lyndale Avenue South
Minneapolis, MN 55409-1499
Pam Fickenscher, pastor
Phone: (612) 827-1074
Fax: (612) 823-1131
John Kerns, minister of music (612) 870-8928
E-mail: onlygrace@wavetech.net
Visit their Web site at: www.spiritgarage.org

Spiritworks
2212 East Carson Street
Pittsburgh, PA 15203
Phone: (412) 488-6629
John S. Bustard, pastor
E-mail: life@spiritworksonline.org
Visit their Web site at: spiritworksonline.org

University Baptist Church
1701 Dutton Ave
Waco, Texas 76706
Phone: (254) 752-1401
Chris Seay, pastor
Visit their Web site at: www.ubcwaco.org

CONFERENCES AND NETWORKS

Alpha of North America. Alpha is a program designed to evangelize seekers. The course materials approach faith from a conservative, modern, evidence-based understanding of Jesus. Its method of no-pressure, small-group discussion and emphasis on experiencing God through the power of the Holy Spirit appeals to Generation Xers. Alpha began at a young urban congregation in London; today the organization holds training conferences worldwide. Contact:

Alpha North America
FDR Station
PO Box 5209
New York, NY 10150-5209
www.alphana.org.

The Leadership Summit. This is an annual event sponsored by Willow Creek Association for church leaders and teams. They "offer all-new material and fresh insights each year" for all churches whether they are "contemporary or traditional." Contact:

Willow Creek Association
P.O. Box 3188
Barrington, IL 60011-3188
www.willowcreek.org

Joy Leadership Center. Trains and supports mainline pastors and lay leaders through conferences, resources, and consulting services. Note the "Building a Church for New Generations" event in March 2000. Contact:

Community Church of Joy
21000 N. 75th Ave.
Glendale, AZ 85308-9622
Tim Wright, director
www.joylead.org

The Vine. An effort to bring together Christians from Protestant, Roman Catholic, and Orthodox backgrounds into creative dialogue about the future of the church and our world, sponsored by Regeneration Quarterly. Contact:

The Vine: An Initiative of The Regeneration Forum
2037 Arlington Terrace
Alexandria, VA 22303
E-mail to: vine@regenerator.com or www.the-vine.org

Young Leader Network. A division of the Leadership Network, a privately funded, nondenominational foundation devoted to connecting church leaders. The Young Leader Network sponsors forums, events and a Web site for those involved in ministry with and to people born after 1960. Contact: www.youngleader.org.

PERIODICALS

Mars Hill Audio. A bimonthly "audio journal" (after the style of public radio) produced by Mars Hill Fellowship, Seattle. Perfect for those who spend a lot of time driving. Although its editorial stance towards pop culture is largely negative, it has produced a helpful report of "Best-Selling Spirituality," also on audio tape. Call 1-800-331-6407 for a catalog.

Mars Hill Review. A journal that "attempts to articulate a refreshing theology of hope," published three times a year with articles on theology, culture, and the arts. See especially the issue on postmodernism, Fall 1998. Call 1-800-990-Mars.

WEB SITES

www.barna.org George Barna research on-line. Lots of good ministry resources.

www.changingchurch.org/perspec/vol19/genx.htm Ministry to Generation X.

www.easum.com/bybill/church21.htm "The Church of the 21st Century" by William M. Easum.

www.elca.org The Web site of the ELCA. Watch for the Young Adult On-Line Project coming soon as the result of Youth and Young Adult Initiative.

www.leonardsweet.com Leonard Sweet's Soul Café is a journal on theology, spirituality, and culture written by the dean of Drew Divinity School. Even the print version has the postmodern style and feel of a Web site. www.sweetsoulcafe.com.

www.leadnet.org Leadership Network connects leaders with other leaders.

www.regenerator.com Regenerator is a journal written by and for "orthodox" Generation X Christians.

www.shootthemessenger.au An Australian site that looks at the connections between Christian faith and pop culture.

www.youngleader.org Connects and empowers young leaders in the postmodern transition.

MUSIC FROM CONGREGATIONS

Cities Vineyard Fellowship
Mark Hjelle
1406 W. Lake St., Suite 208
Minneapolis MN 55408
(612) 825-2512;
E-mail: info@citiesvineyard.com
www.citiesvineyard.com

Community of Life Lutheran Church
Mark Peterson
5453 Firethorn Place
Boise, ID 83705
(208) 385-7020
life@micron.net

Mars Hill Fellowship
Brad Currah
4505 University Way NE, Suite 314
Seattle, WA 98105
(206) 523-3104
brad@marshillchurch.org.

Spirit Garage
John Kerns
c/o Bethlehem Lutheran Church
4100 Lyndale Ave. South
Minneapolis, MN 54409
(612) 827-1074
onlygrac@wavetech.net

University Baptist Church
David Crowder
1701 Dutton Avenue
Waco, TX 76706
(254) 752-1401
www.ubcwaco.org

MUSIC FROM PUBLISHING HOUSES

Augsburg Fortress
P.O. Box 1209
Minneapolis, MN 55440
(800) 328-4648
www.augsburgfortress.org

EMI Christian Music Publishing
Box 5085
Brentwood, TN 37024
(615) 371-4415
www.worshiptogether.com

LIMB Records/Lost and Found
Box 305
Lewiston, NY 14092
(419) 897-9792
www.speedwood.com

Maranatha! Music
P.O. Box 31050
Laguna Hills, CA 92654
(800) 245-SONG
www.maranathamusic.com

Integrity Music
P.O. Box 851622,
Mobile, AL 36685-1622
www.integritymusic.com

Vineyard Music Group
Box 68025
Anaheim, CA 92817-0825
(800) 825-8463
www.vineyardmusic.com

BOOKS

Church leadership

Natural Church Development, Christian A. Schwarz. Carol Stream,
Ill.: ChurchSmart Resources, 1996.

Prepare Your Church of the Future, Carl George. Tarrytown, N.Y.:
Flemming H. Revell, 1991.

The Purpose Driven Church, Richard Warren. Grand Rapids, Mich.:
Zondervan Publishing House, 1995.

Introductions to Christian faith

Finding Faith, Brian McLaren. Grand Rapids, Mich.: Zondervan Publishing, 1999.

The Gospel in a Pluralist Society, Leslie Newbigin. Grand Rapids, Mich.: W. B. Eerdmans, 1989.

The Original Jesus: The Life of a Revolutionary, N. T. Wright. Grand Rapids, Mich.: W. B. Eerdmans, 1996.

Outreach and evangelism

Community That Is Christian, Julie Gorman. Wheaton, Ill.: Victor Books, 1993.

Conspiracy of Kindness: A Refreshing New Approach to Sharing the Love of Jesus With Others, Steve Sjogren. Ann Arbor, Mich.: Vine Books, 1993.

Inside the Soul of a New Generation: Insight and Strategies for Reaching Busters, Tim Celek, Dieter Zander, Patrick Kampert. Grand Rapids, Mich.: Zondervan Publishing, 1996.

Jesus for a New Generation, Kevin Graham Ford, Jim Denney, George Gallup Jr. (Introduction). Downer's Grove, Illinois: InterVarsity Press, 1996.

Reckless Hope: Understanding and Reaching Baby Busters, Todd Hahn, David Verhaagen. Grand Rapids, Mich.: Baker Book House, 1996.

Personal faith stories

Amazing Grace: A Spiritual Vocabulary, Kathleen Norris. New York: Riverhead Books, 1998.

Traveling Mercies: Some Thoughts on Faith, Anne Lamott, New York: Pantheon Books, 1999.

Sociology

Generating Hope: A Strategy for Reaching the Postmodern Generation, Jimmy Long. Downers Grove, Ill.: InterVarsity Press, August 1997.

A Generation Alone: Xers Making a Place in the World, William Mahedy and Janet Bernard. Downers Grove, Ill.: InterVarsity Press, 1994.

GenXers after God: Helping a Generation Pursue Jesus, Todd Hahn, David Verhaagen, Julie Culbreath, Ellen Verhaggen, Daniel Kruidenier. Grand Rapids, Mich.: Baker Books, 1998.

Loose Connections: Joining Together in America's Fragmented Communities, Robert Wuthnow. Cambridge, Mass.: Harvard University Press, 1998.

The Next Generation: Understanding and Meeting the Needs of Generation X, Gary Blair Zustiak. Joplin, Mo.: College Press Pub., 1996.

Out on the Edge: A Wake Up Call for Church Leaders on the Edge of the Media Reformation, Michael Slaughter. Nashville, Tenn.: Abingdon Press, 1998.

Post Moderns, Craig Miller. Nashville, Tenn.: Discipleship Resources, 1996.

The Postmodern Paradigm: Challenges to the Evangelistic Ministry of the Church, Ricky D. Gosnell, 1998.

A Primer on Postmodernism, Stanley Grenz. Grand Rapids, Mich.: W. B. Erdmans Publishing Co., 1996.

The Spectacle of Worship in a Wired World: Electronic Culture and the Gathered People of God, Tex Sample. Nashville, Tenn.: Abingdon Press, 1998.

13th Gen: Abort, Retry, Ignore, Fail? Neil Howe, Bill Strauss, R.J. Matson, and Ian Williams. New York: Vintage Books, 1993.

Virtual Faith: The Irreverent Spiritual Quest of Generation X, Tom Beaudoin. San Francisco, Calif.: Jossey-Bass Publishers, 1998.

Small-group resources

Alpha. See entry above under "Conferences." www.alphana.com.

Augsburg Fortress. Intersections Small Group Series, especially *Starting Small Groups—and Keeping Them Going.* (800) 328-4648.

Crossways International, Minneapolis, Minn. Offers a good Bible survey course.

Serendipity House, Littleton, Colo. 301 level courses are adequate for in-depth small-group resource.

Spiritual gift inventories

Created and Called: Discovering Our Gifts for Abundant Living. Augsburg Fortress. (800) 328-4648.

Finding Your Spiritual Gifts. Gospel Light. (800) 446-7735.

Houts Inventory of Spiritual Gifts. Center for Leadership Development and Evangelism. (800) 804-0777.

Opening Your Spiritual Gifts. Evangelical Lutheran Church in America (Augsburg Fortress). (800) 328-4648.

Spiritual Gifts Inventory. Church Growth Insititute. (800) 553-4769.

Trenton Spiritual Gifts Analysis. Center for Leadership Development and Evangelism. (800) 804-0777.

Worship planning

Contemporary Music Styles, Robert Barrett. 1996, Taylor Made Music, 23608 Via Navarra, Mission Viejo, CA 92691, (714) 457-1892

Guide to Sound Systems for Worship, John F. Eiche, ed. Milwaukee, Wis.: Hal Leonard (Yamaha Corp.), 1990.

Leading the Church's Song, Robert Buckley Farley, ed. Minneapolis: Augsburg Fortress, 1998.

Liturgy Made Simple, Mark Searle. Collegeville, Minn.: The Liturgical Press, 1981.

Reading and Writing Chord Charts, Robert Barrett. 1998, Taylor Made Music, 23608 Via Navarra, Mission Viejo, CA 92691, (714) 457-1892

Virtual Faith: The Irreverent Spiritual Quest of Generation X, Tom Beaudoin. San Francisco, Calif.: Jossey Bass, 1996.

Worship and Outreach: New Services for New People, Donald M. Brandt. Minneapolis: Augsburg Fortress, 1994.

Worship Evangelism: Inviting Unbelievers into the Presence of God, Sally Morgenthaler. Grand Rapids, Mich.: Zondervan, 1995.